Battleground Europe
Mediterranean

MALTA

ISLAND UNDER SIEGE

Battleground series:

Stamford Bridge & Hastings *by* Peter Marren
Wars of the Roses - **Wakefield / Towton** *by* Philip A. Haigh
Wars of the Roses - **Barnet** *by* David Clark
Wars of the Roses - **Tewkesbury** *by* Steven Goodchild
Wars of the Roses - **The Battles of St Albans** *by* Peter Burley, Michael Elliott & Harvey Wilson
English Civil War - **Naseby** *by* Martin Marix Evans, Peter Burton and Michael Westaway
English Civil War - **Marston Moor** *by* David Clark
War of the Spanish Succession - **Blenheim 1704** *by* James Falkner
War of the Spanish Succession - **Ramillies 1706** *by* James Falkner
Napoleonic - **Hougoumont** *by* Julian Paget and Derek Saunders
Napoleonic - **Waterloo** *by* Andrew Uffindell and Michael Corum
Zulu War - **Isandlwana** *by* Ian Knight and Ian Castle
Zulu War - **Rorkes Drift** *by* Ian Knight and Ian Castle
Boer War - **The Relief of Ladysmith** *by* Lewis Childs
Boer War - **The Siege of Ladysmith** *by* Lewis Childs
Boer War - **Kimberley** *by* Lewis Childs

Mons *by* Jack Horsfall and Nigel Cave
Néry *by* Patrick Tackle
Le Cateau *by* Nigel Cave and Jack Shelden
Walking the Salient *by* Paul Reed
Ypres - **Sanctuary Wood and Hooge** *by* Nigel Cave
Ypres - **Hill 60** *by* Nigel Cave
Ypres - **Messines Ridge** *by* Peter Oldham
Ypres - **Polygon Wood** *by* Nigel Cave
Ypres - **Passchendaele** *by* Nigel Cave
Ypres - **Airfields and Airmen** *by* Mike O'Connor
Ypres - **St Julien** *by* Graham Keech
Walking the Somme *by* Paul Reed
Somme - **Gommecourt** *by* Nigel Cave
Somme - **Serre** *by* Jack Horsfall & Nigel Cave
Somme - **Beaumont Hamel** *by* Nigel Cave
Somme - **Thiepval** *by* Michael Stedman
Somme - **La Boisselle** *by* Michael Stedman
Somme - **Fricourt** *by* Michael Stedman
Somme - **Carnoy-Montauban** *by* Graham Maddocks
Somme - **Pozières** *by* Graham Keech
Somme - **Courcelette** *by* Paul Reed
Somme - **Boom Ravine** *by* Trevor Pidgeon
Somme - **Mametz Wood** *by* Michael Renshaw
Somme - **Delville Wood** *by* Nigel Cave
Somme - **Advance to Victory (North) 1918** *by* Michael Stedman
Somme - **Flers** *by* Trevor Pidgeon
Somme - **Bazentin Ridge** *by* Edward Hancock
Somme - **Combles** *by* Paul Reed
Somme - **Beaucourt** *by* Michael Renshaw
Somme - **Redan Ridge** *by* Michael Renshaw
Somme - **Hamel** *by* Peter Pedersen
Somme - **Villers-Bretonneux** *by* Peter Pedersen
Somme - **Airfields and Airmen** *by* Mike O'Connor
Airfields and Airmen of the Channel Coast *by* Mike O'Connor
In the Footsteps of the Red Baron *by* Mike O'Connor
Arras - **Airfields and Airmen** *by* Mike O'Connor
Arras - **The Battle for Vimy Ridge** *by* Jack Sheldon & Nigel Cave
Arras - **Vimy Ridge** *by* Nigel Cave
Arras - **Gavrelle** *by* Trevor Tasker and Kyle Tallett
Arras - **Oppy Wood** *by* David Bilton
Arras - **Bullecourt** *by* Graham Keech
Arras - **Monchy le Preux** *by* Colin Fox
Walking Arras *by* Paul Reed
Hindenburg Line *by* Peter Oldham
Hindenburg Line - **Epehy** *by* Bill Mitchinson
Hindenburg Line - **Riqueval** *by* Bill Mitchinson
Hindenburg Line - **Villers-Plouich** *by* Bill Mitchinson
Hindenburg Line - **Cambrai Right Hook** *by* Jack Horsfall & Nigel
Hindenburg Line - **Cambrai Flesquières** *by* Jack Horsfall & Nigel
Hindenburg Line - **Saint Quentin** *by* Helen McPhail and Philip Gu
Hindenburg Line - **Bourlon Wood** *by* Jack Horsfall & Nigel Ca
Cambrai - **Airfields and Airmen** *by* Mike O'Connor
Aubers Ridge *by* Edward Hancock
La Bassée - **Neuve Chapelle** *by* Geoffrey Bridger
Loos - **Hohenzollern Redoubt** *by* Andrew Rawson
Loos - **Hill 70** *by* Andrew Rawson
Fromelles *by* Peter Pedersen
Accrington Pals Trail *by* William Turner
Poets at War: Wilfred Owen *by* Helen McPhail and Philip Gue
Poets at War: Edmund Blunden *by* Helen McPhail and Philip G
Poets at War: Graves & Sassoon *by* Helen McPhail and Philip G
Gallipoli *by* Nigel Steel
Gallipoli - **Gully Ravine** *by* Stephen Chambers
Gallipoli - **Anzac Landing** *by* Stephen Chambers
Gallipoli - **Landings at Helles** *by* Huw & Jill Rodge
Walking the Italian Front *by* Francis Mackay
Italy - **Asiago** *by* Francis Mackay
Verdun: **Fort Douamont** *by* Christina Holstein
Zeebrugge & Ostend Raids 1918 *by* Stephen McGreal

Germans at Beaumont Hamel *by* Jack Sheldon
Germans at Thiepval *by* Jack Sheldon

SECOND WORLD WAR

Dunkirk *by* Patrick Wilson
Calais *by* Jon Cooksey
Boulogne *by* Jon Cooksey
Saint-Nazaire *by* James Dorrian
Normandy - **Pegasus Bridge/Merville Battery** *by* Carl Shillet
Normandy - **Utah Beach** *by* Carl Shilleto
Normandy - **Omaha Beach** *by* Tim Kilvert-Jones
Normandy - **Gold Beach** *by* Christopher Dunphie & Garry Johnso
Normandy - **Gold Beach Jig** *by* Tim Saunders
Normandy - **Juno Beach** *by* Tim Saunders
Normandy - **Sword Beach** *by* Tim Kilvert-Jones
Normandy - **Operation Bluecoat** *by* Ian Daglish
Normandy - **Operation Goodwood** *by* Ian Daglish
Normandy - **Epsom** *by* Tim Saunders
Normandy - **Hill 112** *by* Tim Saunders
Normandy - **Mont Pinçon** *by* Eric Hunt
Normandy - **Cherbourg** *by* Andrew Rawson
Das Reich – **Drive to Normandy** *by* Philip Vickers
Oradour *by* Philip Beck
Market Garden - **Nijmegen** *by* Tim Saunders
Market Garden - **Hell's Highway** *by* Tim Saunders
Market Garden - **Arnhem, Oosterbeek** *by* Frank Steer
Market Garden - **Arnhem, The Bridge** *by* Frank Steer
Market Garden - **The Island** *by* Tim Saunders
Rhine Crossing – **US 9th Army & 17th US Airborne** *by* Andrew
British Rhine Crossing – **Operation Varsity** *by* Tim Saunder
British Rhine Crossing – **Operation Plunder** *by* Tim Saunde
Battle of the Bulge – **St Vith** *by* Michael Tolhurst
Battle of the Bulge – **Bastogne** *by* Michael Tolhurst
Channel Islands *by* George Forty
Walcheren *by* Andrew Rawson
Remagen Bridge *by* Andrew Rawson
Cassino *by* Ian Blackwell
Anzio *by* Ian Blackwell
Dieppe *by* Tim Saunders
Fort Eben Emael *by* Tim Saunders
Crete – **The Airborne Invasion** *by* Tim Saunders
Malta *by* Paul Williams

Battleground Europe
Mediterranean

MALTA

ISLAND UNDER SIEGE

Paul R. Williams

Pen & Sword
MILITARY

First published in Great Britain in 2009 by
Pen & Sword Military
an imprint of
Pen & Sword Books Ltd
47 Church Street
Barnsley
South Yorkshire
S70 2AS

ISBN 978-1-84884-012-6

A CIP catalogue record for this book is available from the British Library.

Typeset in Palatino

Printed and bound in the United Kingdom by CPI

Pen & Sword Books Ltd incorporates the imprints of Pen & Sword Aviation, Pen & Sword Maritime, Pen & Sword Military, Wharncliffe Local History, Pen and Sword Select, Pen and Sword Military Classics and Leo Cooper.

For a complete list of Pen & Sword titles, please contact
Pen & Sword Books Limited
47 Church Street, Barnsley, South Yorkshire, S70 2AS, England
E-mail: enquiries@pen-and-sword.co.uk
Website: www.pen-and-sword.co.uk

CONTENTS

INTRODUCTION

CROSSROADS

> *With Malta in enemy hands, the Mediterranean route would be completely closed to us.... this tiny island was a vital feature in the defence of our Middle East position.*

Malta's soil never witnessed any great infantry battles and no heavy tanks ever rumbled down its dusty roads. The sky, the seas and the hearts and minds of the people were Malta's battleground, but Winston Churchill was in no doubt that, without this tiny group of islands, Britain's ultimately successful World War II campaign in North Africa would have been impossible to sustain – but why, throughout the ages, has this relatively small archipelago in the middle of the Mediterranean been such a sought after piece of real estate?

There are seven islands but only Malta and its smaller sister Gozo have a year-round population and, of the others, only Comino and Filfla are large enough to justify a prolonged visit. But the answer isn't

Strategically positioned mid-way between Gibraltar and the Suez Canal and on route to British bases in North Africa the island of Malta was a prime target for the Axis forces.

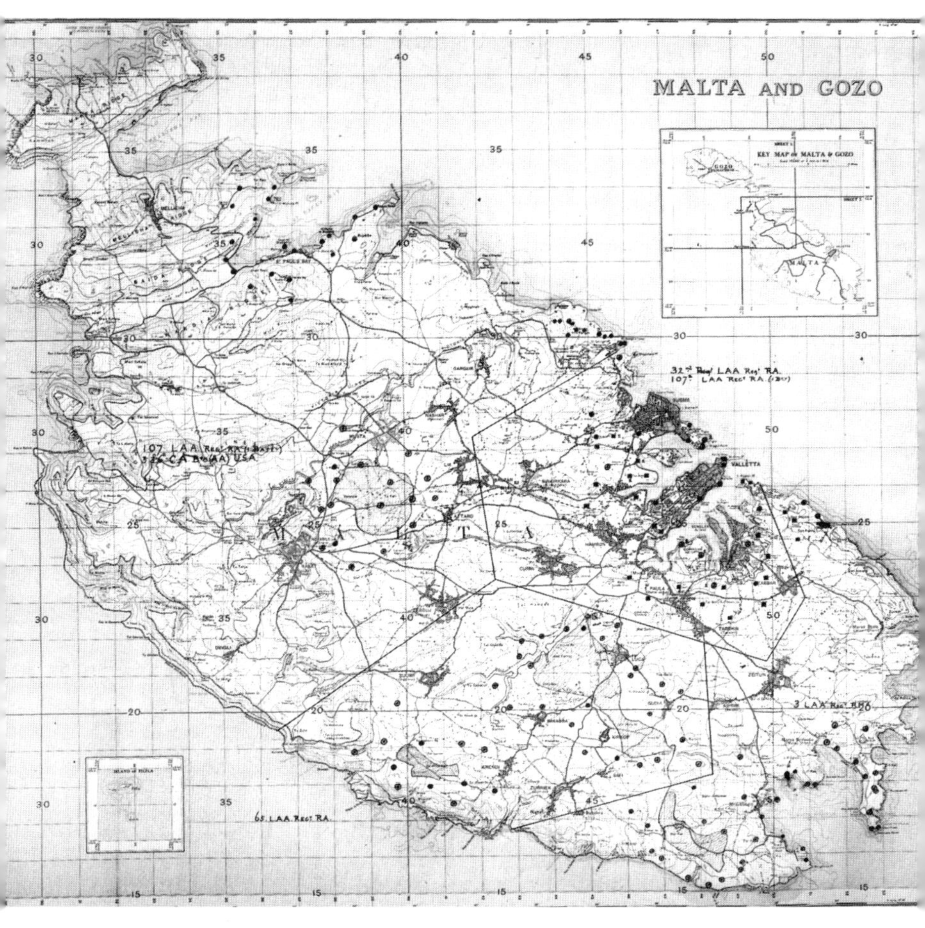

Because of the close proximity of Axis airfields in Sicily and Italy, Malta was subjected to heavy aerial bombardment. The wartime map shows the positions of anti-aircraft guns sited to best defend the island.

solely geographic – though it's not difficult to see how easy it would be for a relatively modest garrison to control the major Mediterranean shipping lanes which still, to this day, are forced to pass within hailing distance of Malta – but also cultural.

This is the point after all, where southern Europe meets North Africa, where Western Europe casts an eye to the Middle East and where devout Christianity borders the Muslim world. Those very facts are at the heart of a turbulent and violent history, which will be fully examined in the opening chapter. But, firstly, let's look at how the Maltese Islands came to be.

Formed as part of a land ridge which ran under the waves from Sicily to Tunisia, Malta was submerged until approximately six million years ago when massive tectonic activity, known as the Messinian Event at the western end of the then land-locked Mediterranean led to an overall fall in the level of the sea due to the widening of the Straits of Gibraltar. The islands' predominantly limestone features have been found to contain the fossils of sea creatures which pre-date history, while the exploration of caverns have uncovered the bones of elephant, hippopotami and antelope, suggesting a land link, albeit a tenuous one, to the African continent remained long after the dinosaurs became extinct.

Civilisation arrived at the island approximately two thousand years before the birth of Christ but it wasn't until the Phoenicians began to use Malta as a trading post that the islands' true potential began to be realised. A springboard for regional domination, yes, but also a trading post, supply base and refuge.

In common with many other tongues, including Hebrew, Arabic, Cyrillic, Latin and most of the modern Western languages, Maltese (or Malti to give the language its correct name) is thought to have its basis in Phoenician-Punic script of which early examples have been found on the island. More on the Phoenicians will follow but it's also difficult to ignore the influence of both the Arabs and the Italians on the Maltese

Valletta in the nineteenth century with its Napoleonic style fortress.

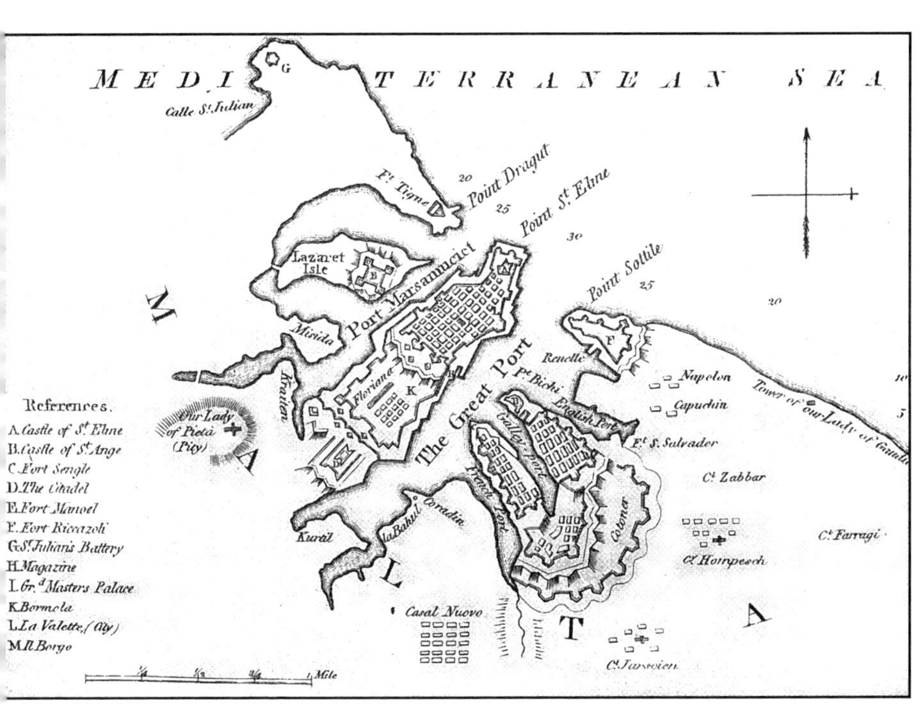

In 1798, while on his way to Egypt, Napoelon Bonaparte occupied Malta, causing the British to begin a blockade which lasted for two years. The Treaty of Amiens directed that the island be handed back to the Knights of St John, who had ruled Malta since 1530. However, the British considered the island to be of too strategic an importance and retained possession. Admiral Nelson was to write:

> ***...I consider Malta as a most important outwork to India, that it will give us great influence in the Levant and indeed all the southern parts of Italy. In this view I hope we shall never give it up.***

language. The Phoenicians were undoubtedly among the first to realise, however, that the straits between Malta and the island of Pantelleria to the west was the gateway to a whole new world.

From the Romans through to Napoleon, many regional 'superpowers' spent time on Malta, but it was the British who were in control when arguably the most significant period in the islands' history began with the construction and opening of the Suez Canal in 1869. Suddenly, ships no longer had to make the perilous 3,000-mile journey around the Horn of Africa to reach the lucrative ports of the Middle and Far East and Malta was the natural stopping-off point for vessels traversing the Mediterranean en route to Alexandria or Gibraltar and beyond. Trade boomed yet, despite the construction of a railway, the island of Malta remained largely unchanged and unsophisticated up until the 1930s except, of course, around the busy Grand Harbour; however its darkest days and finest hours were only just over the horizon.

It was the British who brought the railway to the island in the 19th Century.

Many Maltese place names have had several variations in spelling, usually dependent on which colonial power happened to be 'in residence' at the time, and there is also a modern inclination to abbreviate towns and villages on maps, in road signs, etc.

For simplicity's sake and to avoid confusion, not least to myself, I have tried adhering to one spelling of the likes of Birzebugga, Barrakka and Ta'Qali , while it should also be remembered that places such as Vittoriosa, Senglea and Kalkara can also be known locally by their old names Birgu, L-Isla and Bighi. I'm not saying this book uses the correct derivations, but they are the ones with which I am most familiar.

Paul R Williams
DONCASTER 2008

Valletta Harbour (viewed from the Old Saluting Battery) during the reign of Queen Victoria. Malta was an important staging post for troop ships taking soldiers to police the far-flung posts of the mighty British Empire.

Chapter One

MALTA – A HISTORY OF CONFLICT

TO UNDERSTAND THE COURAGE and fortitude shown by the Maltese people in the face of overwhelming adversity during World War II, it is necessary to delve into Malta's turbulent and violent past.

Regardless of baking summers and an apparent lack of natural resources, the islands' unique situation has attracted more than its fair share of conquerors, despots and tyrants over the years, all largely viewing Malta in strategic military terms - but this wasn't always the case. On a timeline alongside other ancient cultures, one can trace when construction began on the Great Pyramid at Giza – and then wind the clock back a thousand years to discover man was already building a legacy on Malta.

Approximately 5000 BC, and long before these sun-drenched islands found themselves at the centre of the war between Rome and Carthage, 'modern' civilisation already had a toe-hold on this rocky set of islands. In 1865, close to the modern-day town of Birzebugga, English scientist Arthur Issel, searching for fossils, uncovered what is believed to be among the earliest evidence of ordered society in Europe in the caves of Ghar Dalam. But it wasn't until around 3800 BC, during the Neolithic period, that the local populace began to make their mark on the landscape above ground. While tribes in Britain were still hollowing out a basic existence, something far more significant and exciting was taking place on Malta's rocky

Ruins of early settlements on the southern coastline of the island.

southern shoreline. Whatever prompted the new arrivals, shepherds, farmers and fishermen (believed to have migrated from Sicily as finds have been linked to similar at Syracuse) to put down roots and impose their advanced culture on their surroundings, it also inspired them to undertake engineering projects that put Stonehenge to shame in their complexity.

A series of temples and shrines were built, devoted to the gods of fertility, presumably to help them turn the rocky outcrop into something worth cultivating. So advanced were they that the edifices still have archaeologists and engineers scratching their heads in disbelief in the 21st century. Also linked to the alignment of sun and moon, the complexes at Mnajdra and Hagar Qim, probably the best examples remaining nowadays, were also believed to be linked to activity on the islet of Filfla, where settlements may have also existed around this time. Sites at Tarxien, Ta' Hagrat and Skorba are others worth a visit if time allows.

The underground Hal Saflieni Hypogeum at Paola was carved out of 2,000 tons of rock around 2500 BC and is once believed to have contained the remains of 7,000 people. It was also thought to have doubled as a sanctuary, the concept of which was to aid and comfort the Maltese people more than 5,000 years later. This was, however, to prove the last major project this ancient and mysterious race would undertake, before they

Hal Saflieni Hypogeum at Paola thought to have once contained the remains of 7,000 people.

pretty much disappeared off the historical map, by the time the Phoenicians arrived around 800 BC.

Little evidence of their occupation of the islands survives, though locals will tell you a ruined temple could once be found dedicated to the god Melkart in the hills surrounding the fishing village of Marsaxlokk and another on the site of Fort St Angelo overlooking Grand Harbour, but some artefacts have been discovered on wrecks around the shoreline which have led historians to believe many of these seafarers did set up a temporary home on Malta.

The Phoenicians, who originated from the lands north of Palestine now belonging to Lebanon, were essentially traders who are believed to have travelled as far as Britain and Spain for metals which they processed in factory-like workshops in the ancient cities of Sodom and Tyre. Dubbed 'the people of the purple cloth' by the Greeks because of their traditional Royal Purple attire, after colonizing Cyprus, North Africa and Sicily, they named their island colony Mlt, or in modern-day language Malat, hence Malta. The Phoenicians hung around for approximately 600 years but a lack of concentrated archaeological finds suggests they never established a major base on the islands (the rock-hewn sanctuary at Ras-il-Wardija on Gozo is probably the only accessible example of architecture) and their power base had, in the interim, been switched from Lebanon to Carthage in Tunisia.

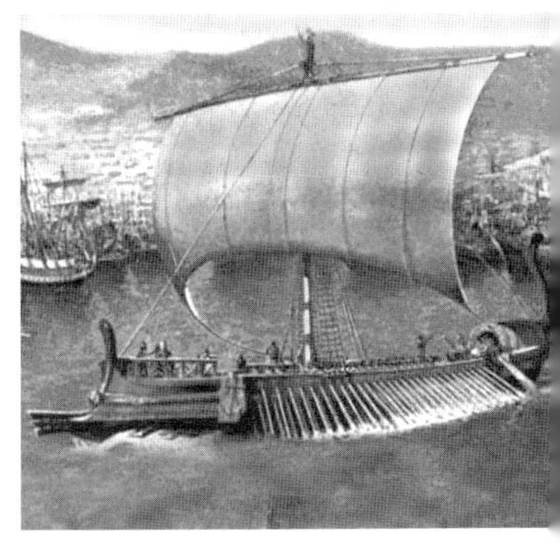

Phoenician trading galley.

One of their great leaders, Hannibal, of course enjoyed famous victories over the Romans in the so-called Punic Wars. But gradually the Carthaginians were worn down and their empire shrank as Rome expanded and, somewhere between 218 BC and 208 BC, the Romans arrived on Malta as the political map of the Mediterranean changed yet again. The island was renamed Melita by the invaders from the north, with a capital of the same name established on the highest point. This was thought to incorporate the whole of modern-day Mdina and parts of neighbouring Rabat, where the Museum of Roman Antiquities (or Roman Villa as it's locally sign-posted) offers a fascinating distraction. Less commercialised and just as interesting, however, is the Roman baths above Ghajn Tuffeija in the north.

Saint Paul's unplanned visit to Malta in 60 AD is, of course, the most significant event during the Romans' reign, not least to the people of Malta

St Paul shipwrecked on Malta in 60 AD.

itself. Shipwrecked when under arrest the apostle, according to legend, made landfall on a tiny islet outside St Paul's Bay. He stayed for three months and, in that time, converted the population to Christianity and reputedly healed the father of the Roman governor Publius, who went on to become the first bishop of Malta. The account can be found in the Bible in the Acts of the Apostles, beginning at chapter 27, verse 39 to the end; then chapter 28 verses 1 to 10. San Pawl Milqi in Burmarrad and St Paul's Grotto in Rabat also cover this account.

With Rome's decline and collapse, Malta entered its own 'Dark Ages' when little is known of the size or activities of the population. The Byzantine Empire did briefly establish an outpost, but the islands' next major occupation was by the Arabs in 870. Believed to have arrived, like the ancient civilisation before them, from Sicily rather than North Africa, they were to have a major influence on Malta's agriculture.

Walling/terracing techniques, which are still used to this day, were applied to protect the fragile and thin soil and to allow new crops like cotton, oranges and lemons to be introduced. The ancient Roman city of Melita was reduced in size and fortified walls, known as medina, were built with a surrounding residential suburb, called a rabat, alongside. The twin cities of Mdina and Rabat were born and are probably the originals of many Maltese place names that have their roots in Arabic.

The Arab way of life suited the Maltese and their surroundings at this time and, for 200 years, the teachings of St Paul were forgotten as the islanders embraced Islam. Strong Arabic influences were still evident when the Normans, better known for their expansionism in Northern and Western Europe, pushed south from their stronghold in Sicily and became the new dominant force in 1090.

For thirty-seven years, raids were frequent from the larger island to the north as French nobleman Count Roger battled with the ill-equipped locals. He was little more than a titled pirate, however, and never deemed it necessary to build a permanent base on the island but his son, Roger II, did and slowly-but-surely, Malta underwent integration into the European way of life rather than that of Arab-dominated North Africa.

It was still more than 100 years before Christianity once again became the main religion on Malta, Frederick III Barbarossa eventually imposing his will on the islanders, who were mainly at this time of predominantly Saracen stock. But Malta continued to be squabbled over by a succession of local powers wanting to impose their own brand of feudalism on the land and its people.

The Hohenstaufen from Germany, the French Angevins, the Aragons and Catalans from Barcelona all had their turn as the poverty-stricken population suffered in increasingly wretched conditions. The induction of the *Magna Charter Liberatis* in 1428 went some way towards releasing Malta and Gozo from some of its crippling feudal obligations, but it wasn't until 1479, when Aragon formed an alliance with Spanish neighbours Castile, that some measure of stability was achieved, albeit still under the auspices of elite nobility.

This was the historical period on which Mussolini was ultimately to base Italy's claim to the islands in 1940 as both powers administered Malta and Gozo from Sicily. Governing councils, called Universita, were created and these eventually led to a measure of autonomy for the islands with the establishment of Consiglio Popolare, or Popular Councils. Spanish and Sicilian noblemen were now integrated into Maltese society, but they still maintained their seclusion by ruling from the lofty perch of Mdina. Many of the islands' oldest families still reside there to this very day.

But a period of relative calm was ended in 1530 when the Knights of the Order of St John of Jerusalem sailed into what was eventually to become Grand Harbour. The Knights were searching for a Mediterranean base of operations after being expelled from Rhodes to the east by the Turks eight years earlier. Previous reconnaissance missions had told them that Malta offered excellent facilities (one of the world's largest deep-water harbours and several creeks in which ships could seek shelter) from which to launch an expedition to recapture Rhodes, but there appeared to be little else on the island that would tempt them into a prolonged stay.

But, with Suleyman I leading the Turkish Empire into modern-day Austria and the Catholic Church fearing an attack on Rome itself, Holy Roman Emperor Charles V of Spain ordered the occupation of Malta to try and stem the tide of advance and, in 1565, the first Great Siege began.

The First Great Siege

Between 1940 and 1943, close to starvation, under constant attack and in daily fear for their lives, Malta's heroic population will have taken little solace from the fact that their forefathers had undergone a similar ordeal almost 400 years earlier.

The weaponry that rained down on the island's defenders in 1565 was, of course, not as concentrated or potentially deadly as that unleashed during World War II and it was the Muslim Turks, not the Fascist Italians and Germans who were planning to nullify and capture the fortifications around Grand Harbour. Even for battle-hardened warriors, it must still have been a terrifying ordeal, however, under bombardment from a vastly superior force and with little food and water to sustain them.

The Turks, led by Ottoman Admiral Sinan, had already had one attempt at expelling the Knights from Malta fourteen years earlier. But, dismayed by their lack of success in early skirmishes, attention instead had been turned to Gozo, where the citadel had been swiftly ransacked following the surrender of the garrison. Modern-day Tripoli had followed suit almost immediately as the Knights' influence in the Western Mediterranean was further reduced and the routing of the Christian fleet by Piyale Pasha at Djerba, off the coast of Tunisia, in 1560 seemed to signal the beginning of the end for the Knights of Malta.

In March 1565, the Turks assembled a massive armada, comprising more than 130 galleys, off Constantinople and set sail for Malta. The Spanish mercenary Francisco Balbi di Correggio estimated their number at 48,000 (though other reports list the invading force at no bigger than 16,000) as opposed to just over 6,000 poised to fight for their lives on the island. Of the latter, some 500 were Knight Hospitallers, 3,000 were what we would now term 'militia' from Malta itself, with the remainder largely

Knights of St John defending Malta against the Turks in 1565.

made up of Spanish, Italian, Greek and Sicilian mercenaries.

The Knights had, by now, established their military and administrative power base around Grand Harbour, or Grand Port as it was known in those days, in the townships of Senglea (L-Isla) and Birgu (renamed Vittoriosa). The reason behind abandoning Mdina and Rabat being that maritime operations were now all-important and these were difficult to oversee from the centre of the island. The Turks arrived off Malta on 18 May but, instead of confronting the defenders immediately, dropped anchor at Marsaxlokk, some six miles down the coast.

Allegedly an argument had ensued between the Turkish land commander, Lala Mustafa Pasha, and naval commander Piyale Pasha about the best way to attack Malta. Piyale apparently favoured making landfall at Marsamxsett, north of Grand Harbour, and laying siege to Fort St Elmo, which guarded the harbour entrance. But Mustafa thought that ploy too risky, as it would have put the fleet within range of the defenders' big guns. He preferred to make an advance across the barely defended plains to capture Mdina, before approaching Fort St Elmo from the rear. Mustafa won the day, but the Turks' decision to concentrate all of their firepower on Fort St Elmo was to ultimately weaken their overall position, as they then couldn't muster enough guns to threaten Mdina, which refused to capitulate.

The Knight Grand Master, Jean Parisot de la Valette, was a shrewd and experienced campaigner who knew how to coax the best out of the men under his command. He didn't over-commit his meagre forces as more than 6,000 cannonballs battered at the fortifications of St Elmo. In the end, the defenders in the bastion held out for sixty days but the 150 survivors that surrendered were shown little mercy by local Turkish commander Dragut Reis, who had them executed and their bodies exhibited in an attempt to intimidate those still sheltering in Vittoriosa and Senglea.

Knight Grand Master, Jean Parisot de la Valette.

Buoyed by the unexpected arrival of a further 600 men from Italy, the Knights staunchly repulsed a furious further onslaught on Vittoriosa in July 1565 which claimed the lives of 2,500 invaders, while a simultaneous attack on Mdina also met with stern resistance and faltered.

By September, the Turks had run out of ideas and the will to maintain the siege through the winter and, when a further 250 knights arrived from Syracuse to bolster the defences; they withdrew their forces having incurred losses numbering more than 9,000 men.

Grand Harbour was in ruins, but the Knights still had their power base in the Mediterranean and they moved quickly to consolidate their position. La Valette had learned plenty from his would-be conquerors, who were expert sappers and had used tunnelling as a weapon in their attempts to undermine the fortifications of Vittoriosa and Senglea. So much so that the defenders were often forced to stand in total silence so they could hear if any attempts were being made to bring down the bastions.

The new city was to be named Valletta, after the man who had masterminded the Knights' survival, and it was to be built atop a labyrinth of underground caverns and tunnels that would be the framework of a future defence policy. Malta's soft limestone was the perfect material for both building and tunnelling. The site chosen for the new city of Valletta, Mount Sciberras, already had a network of caves spread over five small valleys, little wider than ravines, and architect Francesco Laparelli was determined to put them to good use. Reservoirs of fresh water, in case of further siege, were incorporated inside the bastions and modern Valletta began to take shape with the digging of the Great Ditch, which still survives, largely intact, to this day.

The Great Ditch and fortifications.

Within thirty years, an impressive fortress, supported by massive buttresses, was near to completion and by 1615 an aqueduct had been built linking Valetta to Rabat to ensure the reservoirs, principally under Fort St Elmo and alongside the Porta Reale at the top of modern-day Republic Street, were not the only source of fresh water for the capital. Almost two hundred years of peace and prosperity followed under the Knights' rule, with the population of Malta increasing ten-fold within that time. An opera house, theatre and university were all founded, but any thoughts of long-term prosperity seemed to end in 1798 when the French invaded.

The French fleet arrived off Valletta on 9 June and requested entrance to Grand Harbour to restock and take on water supplies. This was merely pretence as Napoleon, fearful of growing Russian and Austrian ambitions in the area, had long-since regarded Malta as a potential strategic stronghold to support his campaign to drive the British out of Egypt and ultimately India.

The Knight's Grand Master Baron Hompesch, fearing an attack, decreed that only four vessels at a time were to enter the harbour. But the French seized on this as an excuse to launch hostilities and swiftly attacked key military positions, landing men in Marsaxlokk Bay, on the barren coast between Sliema and Qawra Point and at Ramla Bay on Gozo. Pushing inland, they quickly overran St Paul's and Mellieha to the north and advanced to Mdina. By mid-afternoon of the 10th, Gozo had also fallen and only Grand Harbour and Marsamxett remained under Hompesch's control.

Knight Grand Master Baron Hompesch.

The defenders had no stomach for a battle and surrender was a mere formality. Five days later, Napoleon sailed for Cairo having looted the Maltese treasury to the sum of £600,000, leaving behind a 4,000-strong garrison under the command of Claude Henri Belgrand de Vaubois.

Within days, Malta was split into twelve municipalities, each under the auspices of a newly appointed French judge. Plans were put in place for an all-encompassing education system on the island with the children of the wealthiest families to be shipped to colleges in Paris. Enslaved Turks were also freed and public finances placed under scrutiny but, confused and demeaned, the local population were far from willing to accept these changes and news of Admiral Nelson's victory at the Battle of the Nile encouraged several acts of civil disobedience.

A mob murdered the governor of Mdina and insurgents seized control of the hilltop citadel, routing 250 French reinforcements from nearby Rabat. Locals then recaptured Gozo and the sighting of British Navy frigates off

The French Fleet sails into Malta.

the coast led to panic among the invaders, who took refuge behind the walls of Valletta, abandoning their positions further inland and along the coast. The British ships set up a blockade which was rarely breached in the two years that the French occupied Malta and, out of ammunition and supplies, Vaubois finally surrendered on 5 September, 1800, giving Britain a controlling interest, ratified by the Treaty of Paris in 1814, in the Maltese Islands that she wasn't to relinquish until the 1960s.

The British regarded Malta as a vital link in the Empire, but they didn't appear to impose the same strict form of colonialism on the Maltese as they did on most of their outposts further east. The Maltese church was given free rein with the local population, for example, (as long as they didn't interfere with island politics) and the Maltese language was allowed to flourish, though English quickly replaced Italian as the second language. Relations with Italy were also discouraged, which didn't go down well with the Maltese nobility who still enjoyed close links with Sicily. But by the late 19th century, Malta had become a prosperous and comfortable place to live. It boasted a busy railway line between Valletta and Mdina which incorporated a long tunnel at the Valletta end that was to prove invaluable at a later date and several stations like the one between the hilltop cities of Mdina and Mtarfa and, though the industrial revolution had largely passed it by, there was enough manual work on the island to satisfy the needs of a growing population.

Not even the outbreak of the First World War had a major effect on life. There was a military hospital on the island at Bighi (Kalkara) in Rinella Bay and the islands' imposing fortifications were strengthened, though the curtain walls and ditches that once linked the forts including the Cottonera Lines and Santa Margharita Lines had now been largely dispensed with as it was thought the bastions would be strong enough to stand alone should they ever come under attack. But, with the aeroplane still in its infancy, Malta was situated too far south to be involved in hostilities; though a few Maltese were to serve, and give their lives, alongside the ANZAC forces at Gallipoli.

Malta was granted self-government in 1921 and, until the rise of Fascism in Italy, a posting to its sunny shores was regarded as a pretty idyllic one by most British servicemen. But Mussolini's push into Abyssinia in 1935 was to set the alarm bells ringing across the world and nowhere louder than in the Mediterranean.

Chapter Two

MUSSOLINI – IN PURSUIT OF AN EMPIRE

"Let us have a dagger between our teeth, a bomb in our hands and infinite scorn in our hearts."

BENITO MUSSOLINI

BENITO MUSSOLINI was invited to form a government as head of the Italian National Fascist Party on the last day of October, 1922. He'd seen limited action on the front lines during the First World War but his allegiances were never easy to gauge. Having established a reputation as a staunch socialist he emerged, having been invalided out of the army following a training ground accident in 1917, with far more right-wing views, which he wasted no time in expressing through the newspaper *Il Popolo d'Italia*.

He helped form the Fascisti or Fascist Party in 1919 and his Blackshirts began a campaign of harassment against all parties prepared to oppose them. By 1921, Mussolini had been elected to the Chamber of Deputies and, with his country on the verge of civil war, King Victor Emmanuel III more or less handed him the job of Prime Minister a year later to avoid bloodshed. The King's plan was to have 'Il Duce' form a government in alliance with the rival Socialists and, to that aim, their leader Giacomo Matteotti was appointed deputy leader. But Mussolini desired absolute power and, among allegations of vote rigging in the elections of 1923, Matteotti was assassinated. The alleged murderer was a staunch supporter of Fascism, and Mussolini in particular, but no one was brave enough to suggest the head of government be questioned let alone brought to trial over the killing; Mussolini had his dictatorship by the end of 1925.

He'd already begun a campaign of aggressive nationalism abroad, bombarding Corfu in 1923 and setting up a puppet regime in neighbouring Albania around the same time. Italian interests in Libya were also given increased backing and a naval base was fortified on the Greek island of

Mussolini signs the Lateran Pact of 1929, which brought into being the Vatican City State. The agreement restored the full political and diplomatic power of the Pope.

Leros to give the Italians a platform in the Eastern Mediterranean.

But Mussolini's major coup in the 1920s was to get the Catholic Church to recognise his Fascist government. Again, allegations of cohersion and corruption surrounded the deal which allowed the Vatican City autonomy in return for Papal approval of the new regime, but Mussolini now believed he had *carte blanche* to make Italy a great colonial power alongside its European neighbours, in particular Britain and France.

He chose mineral-rich but undeveloped Abyssinia, modern-day Ethiopia, as the setting to flex Italy's military muscle. A treaty existed between Italy and Ethiopia from 1928, clearly defining borders adjoining Italian Somaliland to the east. But Mussolini's forces quickly put their own spin on the frontiers agreed and by 1930 had built a fort at Walwal, well inside Abyssinia.

Pressuring from Eritrea (also Italian-owned) to the northwest, Italian forces sparked several clashes with the Ethiopians in 1934 leading the defenders to seek help from the League of Nations. This was merely to

Ruler of Ethiopia, Haile Selassie, personally addressed the League of Nations to ask for assistance against the aggressors. Ineffectual as ever, all the League did was to ban arms sales, which did Abyssinia more harm than Italy.

Abandoned by the Great Powers, Emperor Haile Selassie mobilized his army of 500,000 men, the majority of which was armed with spears.

strengthen Italian resolve, however, and emphasise what many world leaders already knew that the League of Nations had no power other than censure and that the wheels of diplomacy, pre-war, ground very slowly indeed. By the time Italy had been branded as the aggressor and the imposition of sanctions considered, Marshall Emilio De Bono had led a force of 100,000 Italians and 25,000 Eritrean troops into Ethiopia from Eritrea, while General Rodolfo Graziani had marched with a smaller expeditionary force across the border from Somaliland – no declaration of war had been served.

Marshall Emilio De Bono.

Ethiopian Emperor Haile Selassie mobilized his army of 500,000 men, but most of his troops were armed with little more than spears and bows and they were to prove little match for the Italians' comparatively advanced armoury. The city of Adowa, scene of a crushing defeat for the Italians in an earlier conflict at the end of the nineteenth century, was among the first to fall, followed swiftly by the holy city of Axum, which was mercilessly looted. The Ethiopians rallied briefly at Tembien, but Mussolini's forces simply upped

General Rodolfo Graziani.

the ante with the use of gas against both military and civilian targets.

Despite signing the 1925 Geneva Protocol, which prohibited the use of such weapons, the Italians deployed between 300 and 500 tonnes of mustard gas during the conflict, taking no steps to reduce the risk of contaminating the general population. Several Red Cross hospitals became clouded in phosgene, which led to news of the atrocities sneaking out under the cloak of secrecy that Mussolini and his generals had tried to impose on the area. Most of the airborne gas was deployed by the three-engined Savoia-Marchetti SM79 Sparviero (Hawk) and SM81, or the Pipistrello, which was to become the *Regia Aeronautica's* workhorse in Abyssinia and later the Spanish Civil War. The Pipistrello was a low-wing monoplane that was also used for reconnaissance and transport but its low speed meant it was particularly vulnerable to fighter attack so it was more often than not used for night-time operations during World War II, especially in North Africa where there were fewer fighter patrols.

The SM79 was a mainly wooden aircraft powered by three 750BHP Alfa Romeo RC34 engines and was capable of carrying 2,200lb of bombs or two torpedoes. But, because of its low-slung design, it was limited as per payload and defensive armament meaning it, too, could only be used in low-risk operations.

Artillery shells were also packed with the chemicals in powder form and it wreaked havoc among the tribesmen and their families caught in the open. Evidence of mass torture and genocide by Mussolini's infamous Blackshirts was prolific, but the international community largely stood by as the Italians marched into Addis Ababa in May 1937 and Eritrea, Ethiopia and Somaliland was renamed Italian East Africa.

By this time, of course, the Italians had also seen action alongside Franco's Nationalists in the Spanish Civil War. SM79s of the 'mercenary' *Avazione Legionaria* operating in tandem with the Heinkel HE111s, Dornier Do17s and Ju52s of the *Luftwaffe's* Condor Legion in the infamous bombing of Basque-held Guernica and Barcelona.

Exiled Ethiopian Emperor Haile Selassie was to stand before the League of Nations and issue a prophetic warning, 'Today it is us. It will be you tomorrow' and in Malta, at least, his words were being taken seriously.

Making ready for war

The Italian invasion of Abyssinia in 1935 had already prompted Britain to strengthen anti-aircraft defences around Grand Harbour, increasing the number of static guns from twelve to twenty-four. But the cover around the docks was still hopelessly inadequate as most of the weapons were of the almost obsolete 3-inch variety.

In pre-radar days, engineers also constructed a revolutionary sound mirror at Maghtab, on the coast road north east of the famous domed church at Mosta. Based on the design perfected on the Kent coast at Denge, this acoustic listening device known locally as Il-Widna, or 'The Ear', was one of five planned for the Maltese Islands but the only one completed before the concept became obsolete. These 'mirrors' were surprisingly effective up to a range of between twenty-five and thirty miles, using the curvature of the construction's walls to concentrate incoming noise. Unfortunately, as aircraft became faster, potential targets were often overhead before they could be identified and 'The Ear' could only spot raiders from the one direction. Maghtab's site survives to this day, ironically alongside a Malta Telecom satellite dish. But the general feeling among army and air force commanders at least was that, should Malta become the target of invasion from a hostile neighbour, that it was pretty much a sitting duck.

Hence, when German troops entered Prague in March 1939 and the Italians crossed the border into Albania a month later, few military chiefs in London, while acknowledging Malta's strategic importance, were wary of committing scarce resources to the island. Understandably, considering the problems of supply and defence. Only the Admiralty appreciated that

Constructing underground shelters on Malta.

Malta in the wrong hands would be a disaster to war efforts in Africa and the Eastern Mediterranean. British merchant shipping had already been given an ultimatum to stay out of the Mediterranean or risk destruction and both the Army and RAF had more pressing worries closer to home.

With Italy still sitting on the fence awaiting the outcome of Germany's *Blitzkrieg* through northern and central Europe, Malta was still in its 'Phoney War'. But, having a proud history, the Maltese were going to make every possible preparation on their own for the real thing if it came. As early as 1935, during Italy's assault on Abyssinia, volunteers were recruited to train as air raid wardens, fire fighters and first-aid personnel. Health inspectors and the military acted as instructors on intensive courses based at the Sacra Infermeria or Knights Hall in Valletta (nowadays part of the Mediterranean Conference Centre) and there were recommendations, in a report compiled by then Maltese Prime Minister, Lord Strickland, that deep air-raid shelters should be dug in the likely target areas. Strickland was, however, a controversial figure in Maltese politics, having frequent clashes with the Roman Catholic Church and his British overlords, and so it may have been largely political that many of his findings were not acted upon. He died in Attard in 1940.

Colonel Burrows, the British Military Attache in Rome at the time, had even suggested that abandoning Gozo to save Malta might be a ploy to buy time, though did advise that further strengthening of air defences and air cover was vital if the War Ministry decided this was not an option.

As the war crept ever closer to Malta, the number of air-raid wardens rose to more than 600 and preparations echoed those that had taken place in Britain a year earlier. Gas masks were handed out to both the military and civilian population as, if Italy joined the conflict, the use of gas as a weapon was viewed as inevitable, while Emergency Defence Regulations were made law by the civil administration.

Meeting in the Tapestry Chamber of the Grand Master's Palace in Valletta, the government was reformed thus:

Governor
Lieutenant Governor
Chief Justice
Legal Secretary
Attorney General
Chief Medical Officer
Chief of Education
Treasurer
Secretary to Government

Various departments were also formed to administer the islanders' more basic needs, including Communal feeding, Demolition and Clearance, Public Works, Utilities, Telephone and Manpower, while Food and

MVSSOLINI HA SEMPRE RAGIONE

Benito Mussolini addresses his victorious troops at the height of his power. It was all 'down hill' for the dictator from then on.

Commerce, Food Distribution, Bread, Milk and Agriculture were also allotted their own overseer.

Training began under mock air raids, mostly in Valletta, with a naval Swordfish imitating an enemy aircraft dropping bombs or gas. Shopkeepers were told to lock up their shops, meaning that anyone inside at the time had to stay there until the all-clear, or raiders passed, signal was sounded and Charles B. Grech in his book *Raiders Passed* describes how wardens and Boy Scouts acted out the parts of casualties and dispatch riders as soldiers ignited gas canisters on the rooftops above his hometown of Sliema. Advance warning of these 'raids' were published in the island's two main publications, *The Times of Malta* and the *Malta Chronicle*, and broadcasts were also made over the Rediffusion (Cable Radio) network. Those lucky enough to have short-wave radio could also pick up the BBC, but many Maltese still listened to the news on Italian State Radio, where they heard the chilling news of Italy's declaration of war.

Won over by the Germans' almost unopposed march across the Seine and through France, Mussolini had finally decided to go along with the 'Pact of Steel' made with Hitler a year earlier.

On the evening of 10 June, 1940, on the balcony of the Palazzo Venezia in Rome, Il Duce addressed a massive crowd, imploring them; "To Arms! Show your tenacity, your courage, your worth!" – The next morning, Malta was in the frontline.

Bersaglieri (sharpshooters) – Mussolini's elite troops.

Chapter Three

DESIGNS ON AN ISLAND

"The assault on Malta will cost us many casualties...but...I consider it absolutely essential for future development of the war. If we take Malta, Libya will be safe."

COUNT UGO CAVELLERO –ITALIAN CHIEF OF STAFF 1940-43

DAY BROKE WITH A SOMBRE GREYNESS over Southern Sicily at around 4.30am on June 11th, 1940 but, around the airfields of Comiso, Catania and Gela, there was to be no dawn chorus only the splutter of engines and the shouts of ground crew preparing for war. Under great secrecy, the *2nd Squadra Aerea* of the *Regia Aeronautica* had been posted to Sicily from its base at Padua eight days earlier and all units of the *Squadra* were to be involved in the first bombing raid on Malta.

Under the command of Colonello Umberto Massini, thirty SM79s of the *34Stormo BT* lifted off from Catania heading for Hal Far airfield, swiftly followed by a second flight of the *11Stormo BT* based at Comiso bound for the dockyards at Valletta. Half an hour later, a further 10 SM79s of the *41Stormo BT* departed Gela airfield with Kalafrana seaplane base as its target. The bombers were to be given cover by eighteen Macchi C200 Saetta (Lightning) fighters of the *79th* and *88th Squadriglia*, which had a range of more than 500 miles, with another three C200s patrolling the skies above Sicily in case of retaliatory strikes. Even with the comparatively slow speed

Ground crew work on a Savoia-Marchetti at a field in Sicily.

Macchi C200 Saetta (Lightning) fighter.

of the SM79s, the sixty miles from Sicily to Gozo only took around an hour, though it took almost as long for the aircraft to group into formation. But it was still long enough for Malta's radar station to pinpoint their position.

Malta had been equipped with mobile radar since March 1939, with an MD1 transmitter and a RF1 receiver mounted on the back of two Crossley trucks and accompanied by a display unit and control trailer. It was the first radar station, designated as a 242 AMES (Air Ministry Experimental Station) but commonly known as Type 8, to be operated outside of the United Kingdom. The 70-foot aerials were positioned on Malta's inhospitable Western shore at Dingli Cliffs, at 718 feet the highest point on the island and close to where the modern-day Maltese Civil Aviation Authority has located its own radar. It had a range of seventy miles, though that fell to about thirty miles if incoming aircraft reduced their altitude. Manned 24 hours a day by nine men working in shifts of three, the fledgling tracking device was often beset with voltage problems which would cause breakers to overload. But it happened to be working perfectly that morning and the alert was swiftly passed to defensive batteries and the scramble

Maltese Civil Aviation Authority radar at Dingli Cliffs.

Malta's mobile radar trailers.

Fuelling up a Sea Gladiator.

Sir William Dobbie.

order forwarded to the Malta Fighter Flight – the enemy was coming!

As late as April 1940, apart from the flying boats at Kalafrana, Malta had no defensive air cover whatsoever despite several pleas from acting Governor General, Sir William Dobbie, who had been forced into the role of Commander-In-Chief when the Governor General, Sir Charles Bonham-Carter, suffered a heart attack and was invalided back to England that same month.

Drastic action was needed, so when AOC Air Commodore 'Sammy' Maynard heard that eighteen Royal Navy Gladiators (seventeen) were in Malta, albeit pre-assigned to the carriers HMS *Glorious* and HMS *Eagle*, he attempted to requisition them for the island's defence. Initially, the Royal Navy resisted but Maynard, a dogged New Zealander who had seen action on the

Gloster Gladiator.

Western Front during World War I, persisted and three out of the four Gladiators (one was kept back for spares) he'd managed to requisition were ready for action at Hal Far when the Italian bombers were sighted at 6.49am.

The Gloster Sea Gladiator was already obsolete when it came into service and few pilots, and even fewer ground crews, were familiar with its eccentricities. The last biplane fighter, the aircraft had had to be un-crated on the waterfront at Kalafrana and towed a mile uphill on, what were and still are, barely cart tracks before reaching Hal Far. It's still possible to retrace that journey by taking the first road after the turn-off to the Freeport container terminal on the outskirts of Birzebugga but Kalafrana base itself no longer exists having been swamped by commerce after the RAF finally withdrew in 1979.

Flying Officer Mick Collins and his team of a dozen fitters and riggers had to work out how struts were bolted to wings and where the countless control cables were attached before the 840BHP Bristol Mercury engines would cough into life. Even then the Navy had to be dissuaded from taking back the Gladiators, but not before Collins and his men had dismantled and re-assembled them one more time. Maynard wasn't blessed with a large selection of pilots to man his aircraft either. There were few qualified airman still on Malta in 1940 after the 202 (Flying Boat) Squadron had been transferred to Gibraltar at the end of 1939, but Flight Lieutenant George

The *Regia Aeronautica* over Valletta.

Grand Harbour with fires burning in the city after a raid.

Burges, Maynard's personal assistant, was tasked to accumulate what resources were available and eventually seven names were put forward for active duty. They were: Squadron Leader 'Jock' Martin, from the staff at Hal Far, who was to command the flight, Flight Lieutenant Peter Keeble, from the original Hal Far flight, Flying Officer Peter Hartley and Flying Officer John Waters of the No.3 Anti-Aircraft Co-operation Unit, Flying Officer William 'Timber' Woods, ex-Station Flight Hal Far and Pilot Officer Peter Alexander from the radio-controlled Queen Bee Experimental Flight.

During that first raid, the Gladiators' deficiencies became all too apparent. The SM79s had already delivered their payload over Valletta and Hal Far before the Gladiators had gained sufficient height to open fire on the raiders with their .303 machine guns, two of which were in gondolas beneath the wings and another two behind the engine cowling.

Burges gave chase as the bombers circled for the return trip to Sicily, hitting one in the fuselage from long range, the Italian aircraft returning fire with its 12.77 mm Breda-Safat topside gun. But, despite the AA guns dotted around the aerodrome shooting down one raider, the British pilots were left frustrated and new tactics were clearly needed to offset the Gladiator's lack of speed, a measly 253 mph despite the 'boosters' that had been fitted, and agility. It was decided on landing, therefore, that the pilots would have to sit in the aircraft on the runway while on stand-by. The reasoning being that the extra minute gained would allow them to engage the Italian bombers before they'd pushed home their attack. Summer heat would make this uncomfortable for the pilots, who required constant replenishment, but 'Jock' Martin could see no other way in which the Gladiators could compete on a more-or-less level playing field.

It's estimated sixteen small 110kg bombs had landed on Hal Far, causing minimal damage. But the raid on the Valletta area had had more serious implications. Having had close links with Italy, and Sicily in particular, for hundreds of years, most Maltese struggled to come to terms with the fact that its near neighbour had launched a bombing raid from the island where many islanders still had friends and relatives.

Fort St Lucian.

Many Maltese were returning home from, or on their way to, Early Mass as the warning sounded and there was a mixture of shock, indignation and total panic as policemen, in their improvised tunics and armbands, weaved in-and-out of the populace, trying to make their whistles heard among the shrieks and shouts of parents in Sliema, Valletta and the Three Cities of Cospicua, Vittoriosa and Senglea, who were attempting to herd curious children indoors and far away from the glass-fronted verandahs which are still so popular in this area of Malta.

Fort San Leonardo.

The percussion of the four 3.7in guns on Fort Manoel echoed around the normally silent streets, adding to the cacophony, and was joined by the 10 AA guns of HMS *Terror*, which was berthed close to the submarine base on Manoel Island. Gunfire, too, was now coming from Fort Tigne.

Coast artillery had always played an important part in the defence of an island fortress like Malta. Normally, the fleet would provide a strong line of defence but when the ships were away from their station, the garrison had to be able to defend itself and, once the French had been expelled, the British set about adapting Malta's ancient fortifications to their own needs, reinforcing sites like Fort San Leonardo, Fort St Lucian and Fort Campbell and arming the bigger batteries in the 1860s with 24 pounders as well as mortars so the forts were able to command a field of fire both out to sea and inland. A concentric ring of wholly independent forts ringed the naval dockyards and arsenal adjoining Grand Harbour and many of them were to remain operational until the 1950s, though they did, of course, offer large targets to bombers.

The spreading of fear, rather than concerted damage, appeared to be the Italian aim in that first attack, and there is no doubt they succeeded on that score. But six bandsmen of the 1st Coast Regiment, including sixteen-year-old Philip Busittil, acting as observers for the Harbour Fire Control, were

AA barrage around Grand Harbour.

killed in Fort St Elmo (visitors can still see a small plinth erected in their honour) when their position took a direct hit and, in Pieta, Mrs Nina Farrugia and her two young sons Joe and Ninu became the first civilian fatalities of the bombing while several children were among a number of wounded civilians.

More than 140 bombs had been dropped by the Regia Aeronautica in the opening salvo and more raids were to follow that first day. Another fifteen SM79s attacked Kalafrana, the same number headed for Grand Harbour while eight returned to Hal Far. No Gladiators were scrambled this time, but the AA barrage around Grand Harbour was intense and eight Italian bombers were hit. Casualties on the ground continued to grow, seven civilians died when a house in Ponsonby Street, Gzira was destroyed and walls and a roof had collapsed when a bomb landed in the garden of the Modern Imperial Hotel in Sliema.

Laurence Mizzi in *When War Broke Out*, (translated by Joseph Falzon), recorded the testimony of Sliema seminary student, later Parish Priest, Adolf Agius,

> *I was putting my clothes on before leaving for 7am Mass when I heard the sirens signal the first air raid of the war. The wailing of the sirens had barely died away when the San Giocomo anti-aircraft battery opened up; I remember breaking out in a sweat with terror and thinking "This is it! We are all going to be killed." Later on in the day there was another air raid and some bombs fell in the neighbourhood (Palm Street). We all slept under the table that night, except my father who lay on the table. I could not help being reminded of the Pope lying in state. My father was not amused.*

There were thirty civilian deaths that day, with 120 wounded as bombs fell on Hal Far, Bormla, Gzira, Zabbar, Sliema, St Elmo, Msida, Pawla, Pieta and Guardamangia.

Flying Officer Woods did record the Gladiators' first kill later, shooting a Fiat CR42 biplane that was acting as an escort. The CR42 was agile, owing to its double-wing configuration and it had an air-cooled supercharged engine, that was quite revolutionary in its day. But its lack of armour made it vulnerable and it also operated without radio equipment, which made it unpopular with pilots.

A Fiat CR42 having its guns zeroed.

That was the defenders' only piece of good news however and, by the time the 'Raiders Passed' signal had been raised that evening, everyone from Pawla to Pieta knew that war had arrived on their doorstep.

First line of defence

The Italians' decision to target Hal Far airfield on that opening day was understandable as it was regarded as Malta's principal base at that time and, of course, the Gloster Gladiators flew from and were serviced there. Hal Far adjoined the seaplane base at Kalafrana in the southwest of the island and had been first commissioned in the 1920s as a shore base for carrier aircraft. Fairy 3Fs, Flycatchers, Hawker Demons and Wildebeeste supplemented the carrier aircraft occasionally, but when Air Commodore Maynard surveyed his assets before that first raid, he must have despaired.

Nowadays, access to Hal Far is limited. Post-war officers' quarters remain largely intact outside what was the old entrance but these are now home to a number of government agencies. The base itself has been turned into a freight depot and terminal for nearby Luqa, though some sections of the airfield have been turned into an emergency shelter for refugees from North Africa who have been arriving on Malta in increasing numbers since the dawn of the new Millennium.

At the start of the war, Hal Far had four runways, three of which were extended during 1941 to accommodate increased aircraft numbers and the arrival of the heavier bombers. Most of the infrastructure was sited at the northern end of the base, including the fuel dump, though the bomb store was located at the southern tip. Hal Far's problem was that its stony surface was vulnerable to flooding during the rainy season between December and March, as was Ta'Qali.

Ta'Qali had been built on the bed of a long-forgotten lake on the flat plain beneath the ramparts of Rabat and Mdina. Civil airliners had used it pre-war, but the grass surface of its four runways meant it couldn't handle heavier aircraft as the surface deteriorated quickly in bad weather. On the plus side, however, the ground dried out quickly under the sun and engineers were able to utilise the adjacent hillside to provide cover for personnel and its vital fighter contingent, cutting through the rock to create bomb shelters though not, as the Luftwaffe were to believe, building pens for aircraft and munitions beneath the cliff.

Ta'Qali the best preserved of Malta's wartime airfields.

With Luqa, and to a lesser extent Hal Far, having been transformed into an international airport, Ta'Qali remains the best preserved of Malta's wartime airfields as many of the Nissan huts were turned into workshops and outlets for the formation of a

Reconnaissance above Ta'Qali.

craft village and one can still see evidence of the later runways and taxiways around the site. One is an overspill car park for the newly built Ta'Qali National Stadium and is opposite the gates of the soon-to-be-extended national park. Given the restrictions of the other two airfields, it was no surprise that Luqa swiftly became Malta's principal base of operations during World War II eventually, of course, being developed into the impressive international airport that we see today.

Flight Lieutenant George Burges, one of Malta's 'Few', was ironically the first pilot to fly into Luqa when it was opened in June 1939 – he wouldn't recognise the airfield today. Luqa is only a mile and a half, as the Spitfire flies, from Grand Harbour so provided a fast-response base to defend Valletta, but it hadn't been an easy job to construct. Hills had to be flattened and quarries filled in before its three tarmac runways could be laid, but it was well defended with several machine-gun posts built into the perimeter and a taxiway linking it to Hal Far was built so aircraft could be dispersed given fore-warning of a heavy raid. By the time the war was over, Luqa was capable of accommodating more than twenty Wellington bombers, which was some achievement considering its humble beginnings.

There were three other airfields on Malta, but Marsa racecourse (which still stands today, forming part of the Marsa Sports Complex alongside the island's only golf course) was only an emergency landing strip, and Safi (now part of Malta's International Airport) and Qrendi were satellite fields for Luqa. Gozo had an airfield at Xewkija, but it only had a short life span being constructed by the Americans prior to the invasion of Sicily and was decommissioned in August 1943.

Defence of these airfields was basic as the authorities quickly realised they would be overrun should an invading force ever secure a bridgehead, but the principal bases were surrounded by barbed wire and Bren gun carriers mounted patrols, while officers and senior NCOs were issued with pistols, though they were only allowed six rounds of ammunition that had to be returned when off-duty. The lack of ammunition was to cause defenders a severe problem throughout the war and it was not unknown, particularly when the Germans became involved, for enemy pilots to touch down briefly on Malta's airfields and taunt the AA gunners, whom they knew to have used up their ration of ammunition for the day.

A more unorthodox method of defending the airfields was to litter the runways at night with junk to prevent airborne troops landing undetected. Most commonly, trucks and staff cars were used but it was not unknown for packing cases and even wardrobes and drawers (often containing some unfortunate airman's belongings) to be discovered at first light.

Chapter Four

THE LONG HAUL

HAVING FIRED THEIR OPENING SALVO, the Italians didn't follow up immediately. On the 12th June, a lone reconnaissance aircraft, a SM79 of *216 Squadriglia*, in a single sortie over Malta was shot down by Flight Lieutenant Burges (the pilot and observer being rescued in St Thomas Bay) and, though there were four warnings, only two attacks took place on 13 June. Two people were killed at Kalafrana, but a second assault ran straight into the Gladiators patrolling over the north of the island and they jettisoned their bombs over the coastal village of Mellieha, narrowly missing a farmer and his donkey. It was becoming increasingly obvious, however, that the Gladiators were going to make little impact on the SM79s in the long run, even if their luck held out.

By now Flying Officer John Waters had famously christened the biplanes 'Faith, Hope and Charity', the three great virtues of Christianity according to Malta's patron apostle St Paul. This, more than anything, endeared the Malta flight to the islanders but the biplanes needed more than a wing and a prayer if they were to soften the punishment the people of Malta were taking. The Italian bombers had even developed counter measures to thwart the Gladiators, one plane in a formation of six acting as a decoy to lure the less mobile British fighter under the swivel guns of the SM79s.

Sir William Dobbie telegraphed the war office in London, pleading for a force of Hurricanes to help break up bomber formations. Sir Andrew Cunningham, Commander-in-Chief of the Mediterranean Fleet, gave his backing, and on 18 June a squadron of Hurricanes was sent out to Malta. Only four arrived, however, due to mechanical problems and adverse weather and, of those, two were immediately ordered to Egypt.

The situation on the ground was no better. Following the first day of bombing, many of the residents of areas surrounding Valletta and the Three Cities had stayed put, sheltering under anything that gave them some degree of comfort and safety. But by daybreak on 12 June, a mass exodus was underway towards the countryside. It is said that 100,000 refugees formed a slow-moving line leading from Cospicua to Zabbar Gate, also known as Notre Dame (now the headquarters of the Malta Heritage Trust), though a more accurate figure is probably around 70,000.

Those more fortunate were on buses, in cars or on horse-drawn carts. Kathleen Burke, an English teacher in Valletta, describes the scene in David

G. Williams' *The Siege of Malta 1940-44*: 'Every car in the district was chartered, and motors, donkey carts and trucks piled high with furniture filled the narrow streets.'

But the majority were on foot, pushing their belongings in prams or on makeshift handcarts. Many of the women carried bundles on their backs and babes in their arms, as Joseph Micallef describes in *When Malta Stood Alone*;

> *Some of the Cottonara ARP staff was detailed to control the walking refugees by making them keep to the left of the road leaving the right side clear for traffic. As each vehicle leaving Cospicua approached Silver Jubilee Gate, it was stopped and the driver ordered to load as many refugees as he could possibly carry, especially women with children in their arms and without the escort of their menfolk.*

This meant, of course, that many who had left their homes didn't end up where they wanted and villages such as Dingli and Siggiewi, which had its population grow three-fold almost overnight, were suddenly struggling to feed their inhabitants. To this end, 'Economical Kitchens' principally funded by the Sunday collections of Malta's churches, were set up to provide basic nourishment to those left homeless by the bombing, with those eligible entitled to 400g of bread and one hot meal every day. Children were rationed to half that amount but were given a pint of milk and one egg to supplement their diet. The Governor also appointed protection officers, based in Birkirkara, to work with the district

This former railway tunnel in the ditch between Valletta and Floriana was used as an air raid shelter. Now used to garage taxis.

committees in finding billets for refugees. Schools, labour clubs and convents becoming semi-permanent shelters in small towns like Qormi, Zebbug and Zetjun.

Not even the bombs could halt washday.

Not all of those living in and around the dockyards could flee, however, some 19,000 workers and their dependents were required to ensure the facilities in Grand Harbour remained open, while others just weren't prepared to abandon their homes and businesses. After all, rent was still collected on properties, whether lived in or not, and a certain amount of looting had taken place even though perpetrators were threatened with the death penalty.

To protect these workers, a network of underground tunnels and shelters were constructed, with others already in place being adapted for use. One such was the disused former railway tunnel in the ditch between Valletta and Floriana, which is now a taxi garage. Individuals were encouraged to excavate their own shelters out of the soft limestone, even using the bastion walls, and several examples of what these looked like are still in evidence today. The limestone would harden quickly in the sea air, but roof falls were common in newly built shelters subjected to a nearby bomb blast and for this reason, most sought refuge in a large communal shelter.

It is possible to gain an understanding of what it would have been like to live in these underground caverns by visiting the Malta at War Museum at Couvre Port in Vittoriosa.

There were eighteen official ARP sites on Malta in 1940 but, along with the Special Constabulary, a warden's duty lay primarily in the enforcement of blackout and curfew regulations and the aftermath of bombing raids in the street.

Shelters had specially appointed supervisors, voluntary at first, who would see to the security of emergency rations, organise medical assistance

Entrance to a former shelter.

and ensure the 'gas' traps were in place during a raid.

As mentioned earlier, there was a real fear that Mussolini would use mustard gas on Malta as he had in Abyssinia some five years earlier and, to this end, all communal shelters were fitted with a 'gas trap' over the main exits. These were often nothing more than woollen blankets soaked in water and tied down at the bottom and sides, however, and would have formed no defence against a chemical attack had the Italians gone down that road. The ordinary Maltese civilian didn't know this, of course, and those blankets remained a comfort to many while the conflict raged.

The shelter at Couvre Port was fairly typical of those constructed around the

Tools used to carve out a communal shelter.

dockyard area in 1940. Chambers were hewn out of the rock using basic tools like picks and shovels. The main entrance stairs being protected by a heavy concrete hood, with a thick blast wall built to ensure any concussion would be partly absorbed and partly deflected away from the main living areas. To construct the chambers within the shelter, two vertical channels would be dug leaving a large chunk of rock between them. This would then be broken up with sledgehammers.

Most would be forced to sleep in bunks built into corridors, though latecomers would often have only the floor and their belongings as a bed unless their family were among the privileged few who could afford a 'private' cubicle.

For a fee of one shilling, wealthier refugees from the bombing could ask the District Commissioner for permission to hollow out their own area, the only criteria being that the extension work had to be completed within three months and had to be set at the same level as all the other rooms off that corridor and there was to be no fixed doors. Families did their best to make some of these rooms a home from home, but they were still subject to the same hardships as everyone else in that the caverns' porous rock allowed water, ankle deep at times, to collect and the electricity supply often failed if a raid hit a sub-station.

Lighting windows were carved out of the rock so candles could provide emergency lighting, but candles quickly became a rare commodity so the Maltese turned to more traditional methods. A hollow in the rock was filled with water and then topped with a film of olive oil onto which a wick set in cork (known locally as a *nichu*) was placed. As the wick absorbed the oil, it provided a cheap and long-lasting light though these, too, became scarce when the supply of cork became subject to rationing and, it's fair to say the fumes they gave off hardly added to the ambience.

Not all chambers were used for living quarters in these shelters as the supervisor had to commandeer a space of his own for his papers and equipment such as a hard hat and fire bucket, while other sections were designated as infirmaries (with a lack of hygiene, the heavy air inside the shelters was an active breeding ground for diseases like scabies, tuberculosis and dysentery), while the Couvre Port shelter even had a first aid cupboard and delivery room.

As there still wasn't adequate advance warning of raids, residents at the bottom of Kingsway (now Republic Street) in Valletta couldn't hear the speakers at the City Gate (formerly the Porta Reale), for example and had to rely on the raising of a red flag above the Governor's Palace. People were understandably anxious not to stray too far from comparative safety. Shanty towns, therefore, would often spring up in the ditches at the entrance to shelters in the Three Cities, which introduced a further hazard to public health.

Sleeping arrangements inside a community shelter.

With problems multiplying, June 22nd brought more black news from the Mediterranean as Vichy France signed an armistice with Germany and, three days later, with Italy.

Malta, and Britain, now truly did stand alone in the Mediterranean.

Lull before the storm

What was strange about the remainder of 1940 was the comparatively low level of casualties (every two raids only claimed an average of one life) among the civilian population considering the perilous state of Malta's defences. Much of this could probably be put down to the wayward accuracy of Italian bombing, but the Maltese infrastructure had also had plenty of time to prepare for war, even though it had almost caught out the military. There were still tragedies, however, and twenty-eight people died when a bus, en route to Valletta, was destroyed at Marsa crossroads and Flight Lieutenant Keeble, one of the Gladiator pilots, was killed in a dogfight with a CR42 of the *74 Squadriglia*, piloted by Sottoten Mario Benedetti. Both machines plunged into the ground at Wied il-Ghajn. Ironically, Keeble was in the cockpit of a Hurricane at the time.

Flying Officer Hartley was also shot down when his Gladiator attacked a SM79 and its nine-strong escort of CR42s of the *75 Squadriglia*. The Gladiator's fuel tank received a direct hit and exploded, forcing Hartley to bail out over Marsaxlokk. He survived to return to England thanks to care received at the Mtarfa Military Hospital, having been rescued by a launch out of Kalafrana, though he received severe burns as he was wearing only his khaki issue in the cockpit due to the oppressive heat.

However, the British had begun striking back at the Italians; the Fairey Swordfish of the Fleet Air Arm, now based on Malta, launched a raid on the port of Augusta in Sicily and also sank a U-boat.

Supplies, too, were still getting through and, on August 12th, Operation

Swordfish aircraft of the Fleet Air Arm began to strike back against Sicily.

Hurry saw twelve Hurricanes, the relatively inexperienced 418 Flight later to become the mainstay of 261 Squadron, alongside Malta's Fighter Flight, set sail from Greenock aboard the aircraft carrier HMS *Argus* to relieve the Gladiators who had, nevertheless, accounted for eleven Italian aircraft in three months. Escorted by the battleship HMS *Valiant* and the cruisers HMS *Coventry* and HMS *Calcutta*, three cargo ships and a tanker arrived carrying 2,000 extra troops, and an eight-ship convoy to evacuate British civilians and dependents arrived safely in Alexandria.

The defences around Grand Harbour received a major overhaul with a boom defence created with a number of heavy chains and nets. A guard ship, HMS *Westgate*, patrolled the entrance, while a second strengthened chain linked Fort St Elmo to Rinella Point on the opposite bank. Several underwater spikes also made entering Grand Harbour a tricky proposition without charts. Also the airspace above Malta had become much more dangerous for raiders. The dockyards and airfields now had 4.5in AA batteries with a range of 40,000ft, and the capability of laying down a box barrage.

September, however, saw a change in Italian tactics and a sound that was to bring terror to the people of Malta in the next three years. Having previously limited their raids to high-level bombing, the *Regia Aeronautica* acquired a squadron of fifteen Junkers Ju87 dive-bombers from the *Luftwaffe*. The infamous *Stuka*, or *Picchiatello*, as it was known in Italian colours, was a newcomer to the war in the Mediterranean, though it had had huge success at the forefront of Hitler's Blitzkrieg across northern

Junkers 87 dive-bombers, a recent acquisition of *Regia Aeronautica*.

Europe, with its built-in high-pitched sirens instilling fear in those on the ground as it began its plunge. The Stuka, which launched its bombs off an 80 degree dive and had an automatic stick return that would pull the plane out of that dive, even if the pilot blacked out under the G-forces, was in its element attacking vehicles, ships or stationary targets, but was cumbersome in the air and vulnerable to more agile and better armed fighters.

First sent out to attack shipping off Malta on 2 September in a mission code named Operation Hats, the *Picchiatello* squadron met with little success but three days later five aircraft, having failed to find their initial target in Grand Harbour, bombed Delimara near Kalafrana and on 12 September a raid was launched on Hal Far. On that occasion Ju87s caused significant damage to the runways before returning to strafe defensive positions and buildings dotted around the airfield perimeter. Gladiators and Hurricanes eventually chased out the raiders to sea, but not before the Royal Malta Artillery's AA guns had shot one down and the Hurricane of Pilot Officer Barber had claimed another.

Barber describes how he claimed his 'kill' over the islet of Filfla in *Hurricanes over Malta* (Brian Cull/Frederick Galea):

> *As I approached, his rear-gunner obviously saw me and he turned to meet me. We did head-on attacks – I was firing and he was firing. We made three head-on attacks and during my last attack my guns ran out of ammo. I whipped round in a turn as we passed and, to my amazement, I saw him losing height rapidly with glycol pouring out of his engine. He wasn't on fire and he landed with a big splash in the sea. He floated actually.*

The Hurricanes' arrival on Malta had been a huge boost to the defenders. Designed by Sidney Camm, the RAF's first monoplane fighter was the unsung hero of Britain's war effort. It was to form the backbone of Malta's fighter squadrons throughout 1941 and 1942 with the Hurricane IIAs supplied to 261 Squadron, based at T'Qali having 12 wing-mounted .303 Browning machine guns and the new, improved Merlin XX engine.

Italy had, by this time, also launched an offensive in southern Egypt and had invaded Greece

The Hurricane, unsung hero of Britain's wartime defences.

but, despite the Hurricanes, they still maintained relative control of the skies over Malta meaning shortages on the ground were inevitable. No sooner had the Maltese come to terms with having no petrol for their cars or taxis, than the Wembley Ice Cream Company had to be moth-balled, depriving locals of their favourite Sunday afternoon treat. Several shopkeepers were also prosecuted for increasing the price of essential goods as the authorities clamped down on privateers.

Italian State Radio was now conducting a war of words as well. Aware that they enjoyed clear reception in Malta, they delighted in informing the people that the *Regia Aeronautica* had shot down several 'Spitfires' (their deployment in Malta was still many months away) and completely destroyed the island's railway network in a single bombing raid, not realising the trains had actually stopped running in Malta eight years earlier!

When a Sunderland Flying Boat confirmed the sighting of the Italian Fleet in harbour, Operation Judgement was planned.

Restrictions were forcing the bus companies to severely downsize operations, though 1940 was to end on a more positive note with the arrival of three more convoys in October and a further four-ship convoy, escorted by HMS *Malaya*, in December. The Colonial Office, in joint agreement with the Governors' office on Malta, was attempting to stockpile six months of rations while the Italians' bombing campaign was only sporadic. But the biggest boost to morale came in November, with the attack on the major Italian naval base at Taranto. A Sunderland, operating out of Kalafrana, confirmed earlier reconnaissance reports from the Martin Maryland of Pilot Officer Adrian 'Warby' Warburton based at Hal Far that a large portion of the Italian fleet was 'at home'.

Martin Maryland.

Warburton was to become a legendary figure in the air battles over Malta. A true son of the islands (he was actually born on board the submarine of his father in Grand Harbour), 'Warby' piloted a Beaufighter and a Spitfire in the defence of Malta as well as his Maryland earning a DSO, DFC and American Distinguished Flying Cross while on secondment to the US 8th Army Air Force. While flying reconnaissance over Germany in 1944 Warburton, then a Wing Commander, disappeared, with his plane only discovered in 2002 in Bavaria. Visitors to the Malta Aviation Museum near Ta'Qali can view the remains of his aircraft.

Pilot Officer Adrian 'Warby' Warburton.

Warburton's twin-engined Maryland had been designed to carry a three-man crew and act as a light bomber. But, relatively quick compared to other aircraft of its size, it was to prove invaluable as a reconnaissance aircraft to the Fleet Air Arm and, later, as a tow for drones. The Sunderland was Britain's most successful flying boat but it had begun the Second World War as a search-and-rescue aircraft, able to carry enough fuel in its six drum tanks to power its four Bristol Pegasus engines for between eight and 14 hours flying time. Its armament was increased when deployed into the Mediterranean theatre, with .303 Browning machine guns added to the tail and the fuselage. It could also carry bombs, mines and depth charges.

The work of Warburton's Maryland and the Sunderland convinced Admiral Cunningham that his Mediterranean fleet could complete a major strike against the *Regia Navale* without suffering much damage themselves. Cunningham was certain his forces would be a match for the Italians in a sea battle but plans had long been drawn up for a seaplane attack on Taranto, code named Operation Judgement, should the opportunity arise and Cunningham was anxious to use the element of surprise.

Operation Judgement did call for aircraft carriers HMS *Illustrious* and

THe possibility of an attack on the Italian fleet at Taranto came about when HMS *Glorious* served as the Mediterranean Fleet aircraft carrier.

'Sitting Ducks' the Italian fleet at Taranto. RAF reconnaissance photographs taken by a Maryland flying from Malta.

HMS *Eagle* to launch their planes in unison. But *Eagle* had been damaged in action and was unable to take part, meaning *Illustrious*, who was to shortly earn her own footnote in Malta's history, accompanied by four cruisers and four destroyers, had to make the attack alone. A total of twenty-one Fairey Swordfish, carrying a mixture of bombs and torpedoes, struck a mortal blow against the Italian fleet that night, with six battleships, including the *Duilio* and *Littorio*, three cruisers and eight destroyers suffering differing degrees of damage, with the battleship *Conte Di Cavour* being effectively ruled out of further action altogether.

Top: A Swordfish launches a torpedo. The attack on the Italian fleet took place on the night of 11 November 1940.

Above: The battleship Littorio down by the bows following the attack.

Below: The battleship Caio Duilio rests on the harbour bottom.

Top: Blackburn Skua, Royal Navy dive bomber.

Bottom: HMS Warspite in the Meditteranean.

HMS *Argus* tried to deliver a further twelve Hurricanes to Malta on 17 November, but, this time, Operation White was to prove something of a disaster. Early November had seen 261 Squadron able to recharge its batteries in general, despite the destruction of an empty hanger at Luqa and a raid on Zabbar, which destroyed four houses, though thankfully without casualties. But the squadron needed replacements so, attempting to replicate her mission of earlier in the year, *Argus* sailed past Gibraltar and into the Mediterranean again and launched two flights of Hurricanes accompanied by two navigating Blackburn Skuas that had also participated in Operation Hurry.

The Hurricanes were to meet up with a rescue Sunderland over Pantelleria, which was to guide them into Luqa but, due to a mix-up over the range of a fully fuelled Hurricane and inaccurate weather reports, the two flights set off too far to the west with only four aircraft from the first flight reaching Malta before they ran out of fuel and none of the second half-dozen Hurricane's making land.

A catalogue of disasters dogged the second flight in particular, starting when the Sunderland they were due to rendezvous with developing engine trouble and not leaving Gibraltar. It was compounded when a Wellington sent from Malta as a replacement failed to find them. The accompanying Skua quickly became lost and, with his radio not functioning, he was unable to summon help. The fighters all dropped out of the sky one by one and the Skua was shot down by Italian anti-aircraft

St Peter and St Paul Bastion. The old customs house is below, left, Upper Barrakka Gardens can be seen above.

HMS *Upholder*.

fire as it circled over Sicily and its crew taken prisoner. The survivors of the mission were forced to land at Ta'Qali with their fuel tanks empty, but four pilots did survive to join Malta's defences.

Nine ships, in two convoys, got through from Alexandria in December and the U-class submarine HMS *Upholder* took up station on Manoel Island to increase Britain's predatory threat to Italian shipping. Even Admiral Cunningham aboard his flagship HMS *Warspite* managed a visit to the island, bringing festive cheer to the thousands who flocked to the Barrakka Gardens above Grand Harbour to greet him.

With 1940 ending on a relatively quiet note and Italian focus elsewhere, (there were no raids between 21 - 28 December), hopes were high that life in Malta was getting back to normal. Cinemas, such as the Capitol in Valletta, and bars reopened, as did the Royal Opera House, while ARPs and British servicemen organised Christmas parties for the children. But the full refugee centres and blackout was a constant reminder that this island was still at war and news then reached Naval Intelligence, via their monitoring station at the Lascaris Bastion near the docks in Floriana, that the Luftwaffe's much-vaunted *Fliegerkorps X* was on the move from Poland to Sicily – an escalation in the siege was just days away.

Chapter Five

THE ILLUSTRIOUS BLITZ

"Illustrious Mussen Sinken!"
ADOLF HITLER

THE BEGINNING OF 1941 had brought renewed hope to the people of Malta and the armed forces defending the island. The Italians were clearly overstretched and that had meant some respite for islanders at the end of 1940, with Mussolini diverting resources further east to support faltering campaigns in Greece, Albania and Yugoslavia and the Italians struggling to make inroads against the British in Egypt. The *Regia Navale* had also been struck an almost fatal blow by the Swordfish raid on Taranto, which had effectively wiped out half of the Italian fleet, and that in turn had opened the door for more convoys to reach Malta via Gibraltar and Alexandria. The RAF was also becoming bolder in their harassing of Axis supply lines between Naples and Tripoli, with Malta rapidly becoming the centre of offensive operations in the Mediterranean, as Churchill and the Admiralty had always hoped it would. Though there were still only sixteen Mark 1 Hurricanes to defend the Maltese archipelago, the same number of Vickers Wellington bombers were operating out of Hal Far and several Martin Marylands, one of which had been so instrumental in locating the Italian fleet in Taranto, flew out of Luqa.

The twin-engined Wellington was ideally suited to the Mediterranean theatre, with its 1,800-mile range sufficient to launch missions from Malta against Sicily and Libya, as well as attacking the Italian convoys.

Malta based Wellingtons were able to strike at Axis targets in Sicily and North Africa. DIGIART by JON WILKINSON

Affectionately known as 'The Wimpy' by servicemen (after Wellington Wimpy in the popular Popeye cartoon), the Wellington was popular with bomber crews as it was able to absorb enormous amounts of damage and still remain airborne thanks to the intricate lattice construction of its fuselage. This did mean that the Wellington took longer to build than other comparable bombers and was less adaptable, but more than 11,000 were built after it was first commissioned in 1936 and its eight .303 Browning machine guns meant it could hold its own in a dogfight en route to delivering its 4,500lb bomb load.

The Lascaris War Rooms, the majority of which are buried deep underground, had also become a vital cog in the intelligence war, intercepting wireless traffic and co-ordinating both attack and defence strategy. But it was obvious that Italian shortcomings in relation to Malta and the Mediterranean in general, would not be tolerated for long by their allies who were still sweeping all before them on their northern and western fronts. Hitler had become increasingly agitated by the Italians'

Entrance to the underground War Rooms at Lascaris.

Above and below: Operations Room at Lascaris.

lack of organisation and ruthlessness. Mussolini had expected the British to sue for peace once France had fallen, allowing the Italians to expand across North Africa and use Malta as a staging post. But the fact that the British had not only dug in but had also begun to attack the Italians on their own doorstep was causing Mussolini many sleepless nights. A change of tactics was clearly called for but it soon became clear that the Italian generals had no 'Plan B' – which was when Hitler ordered in the *Luftwaffe*.

General Hans Geisler.

The *Fliegerkorps X*, under the command of General Hans Geisler, was ordered to Sicily under German War Directive No. 22. With a successful anti-shipping campaign in Norway behind them, the X Air Corps' initial brief was to disrupt British shipping in the Western Mediterranean and effectively make the area between Sicily and North Africa a 'no-go' area for Churchill's Force H, which operated out of Gibraltar as an escort for merchant and military convoys en route from Malta to the Bay of Biscay and vice-versa. But Geisler's orders also included support of Axis troops in Albania and the neutralisation of Malta and the British Mediterranean Fleet.

The advance guard arrived at Comiso on 8 January 1941. It included twenty-nine Heinkel 111Hs, eighty Junker 88As and the same number of Junker 87Rs.

The Heinkel 111 was the mainstay of the Luftwaffe medium bomber

Workhorse of the *Luftwaffe* – the Heinkel III. Being refuelled by use of a hand pump.

Ju 88 arriving on Sicily.

arsenal, a veteran of the Battle of Britain; it was fitted with a rotating bomb rack (capable of carrying eight 250kg bombs) while the Daimler Benz engines on early models could generate an airspeed of 225 mph. During its service with the Condor Legion during the Spanish Civil War, it would often out-run opposition fighters but up against Spitfires and Hurricanes, of course, it didn't fare as well, though by 1941, the He111H had been developed with a new 1,100 HP Junkers Jumo 211 engine (which increased its speed to over 250mph) and had additional gun ports to supplement its original three machine-gun forward-facing armament.

The Ju88 was probably the most versatile of Germany's aircraft in World War II. Used as a bomber, close support escort, night-fighter and reconnaissance plane at various times, it also saw service as a torpedo bomber and fighter. The Ju88 was Goering's pride and joy and was involved in the first raids on British soil in 1939. Capable of around 280mph, it could carry 2,800kg in ordnance but, despite its speed advantage over *Luftwaffe* 'stablemates', the He111 and Dornier Do17, it sustained more losses in the Battle of Britain than both the aforementioned. It was, however, a superb anti-shipping weapon, which was why it was deployed to the Mediterranean.

Commander G.W.G. Simpson arrived on Malta to assume command of the new Royal Navy submarine fleet on 8 January, but just two days later he found himself in the centre of one of the most intense raids so far on the island.

Operation Excess was the name given to a complex passage of four simultaneous convoys, set to dovetail on 10 January. For Malta, that meant supplies on board the MV *Essex*, a refrigerated New Zealand-registered freighter departing from Gibraltar, and the *Breconshire* and *Clan Macauley* out of Alexandria. The *Essex* had arguably the most valuable load, carrying twelve crated Hurricanes as well as seed potatoes and ammunition. All three reached the sanctuary of Grand Harbour more or less on schedule, but their principal escort carrier, HMS *Illustrious*, wasn't so lucky.

***Essex*, refrigerated freight headed for Malta with Hurricane fighters for the island's defences.**

Unfortunately for the British, 10 January also happened to be the day that the *Fliegerkorps X* was to see its first action in the Mediterranean. Shortly after mid-day, some 100 miles to the west of Malta, the *Illustrious* came under fire from two Savoias of the *Regia Aeronautica.* They released torpedoes, but the carrier managed to take evasive action and avoid damage. This, however, was only the prelude. Less than half-an-hour later, a large formation of Ju88s and Ju87s appeared over the horizon. Flying in the familiar *kotten*, or three-plane V formation, the dive-bombers fell on the

HMS *Illustrious* with Swordfish on her flight deck.

Fairey Fulmar.

Illustrious as she was at her most vulnerable. Her Fulmars and Swordfish were in the process of returning to their mother ship and got caught in the frenzy as the German aircraft attacked over the port and starboard bows, braving the barrage of the *Illustrious'* 4.5-inch guns and AA fire.

Inside seven minutes, the carrier had been hit six times with a stricken Ju88 also crashing onto the deck, sparking a raging fire. One bomb struck a Fulmar as it descended the aft-lift, causing a massive explosion below *Illustrious'* armoured main deck, while another crashed straight through a gun turret and out through the hull. It didn't explode but none of the sailors in its path stood a chance. David A. Thomas quotes crew member Shadrack Scommel in *Malta Convoys*;

> *In all my years of service in the Royal Navy the most horrific and the most pleasant memories were with the* Illustrious. *As the bombs fell and exploded, so the aircraft carrier of 23,000 tons started to bounce on the water, bombs bursting all around – three or four hits. One semi-armour-piercing went through the white line painted on the deck of Illustrious straight into the hangar, with enormous loss of life by men who thought it was safe with five inches of armour plating over them.*

The Illustrious lists to port as her crew strive to save the striken carrier.

The ammunition conveyor exploded and virtually everyone in the adjacent wardroom lost their lives. In total, 126 of *Illustrious'* crew were killed and ninety-one wounded, many with horrific burns. The heat was so intense that many of the victims could not be identified. Fire crews fought bravely to control her many fires but Rear Admiral Lyster's flagship seemed doomed, listing heavily due to the amount of water being pumped into her to put out the fires. She'd also lost her steering but, by clever use of her engines, Captain Denis Boyd was able to get her underway again as the Ju 88s and Ju87s headed back to Sicily and, by 9.45pm that evening, she nosed her way gingerly into Grand Harbour.

She portrayed a forlorn sight as she limped toward the Parlatorio Wharf in French Creek, under Corrodino Hill (now the No. 6 Dock of Malta Dry Dock her blackened and blistered hull lit by an eerie red glow within. For a brief moment as she came alongside, workers lining the dockyard wall in Vittoriosa fell silent, too shocked to speak as the smoke from her fires and the stench of death fell across nearby Cospicua and Senglea. Engineers knew they had no time to spare, however, and were on board making damage assessments as a fleet of trucks and ambulances evacuated the wounded to Mtarfa Hospital. They concluded that the *Illustrious'* engines were still operational and, that with some superficial repairs, she could be escorted to Alexandria.

Work began the following morning, as the dead were unloaded onto minesweeper HMS *Fermoy*, moored alongside, for burial two miles out at sea. Unfortunately, a few of the bodies weren't weighted down properly and were washed ashore weeks later on the southern shores of the island. But time really was of the essence as, with one eye on the sky, the Maltese and the Royal Navy set about making the carrier fit for the sea again. They were aided by the weather; daybreak brought a dull, overcast day with rain in the air and a cloud base so low it prevented both the *Luftwaffe* and *Regia Aeronautica* from mounting a raid. The Axis forces had also been hampered by a Wellington raid on Catania the previous night which had destroyed a Ju88, an SM79 and two Ju52s as well as damaging at least half a dozen He111s and MC200s.

As workers swarmed over the flight deck, a roll call took place among the crew. The mood was sombre as names went unanswered or someone reported a friend or colleague 'missing'. As assessment of the *Illustrious'* battle-damage concluded that it was more important to make her seaworthy than operational, the holes in her armoured flight deck, the first of its kind, were largely ignored. But experts were called to repair her steering and navigation system, including gyrocompass specialist Albert Fuller who, along with most naval dockyard personnel, had been billeted at St George's Barracks in Pembroke, north of Sliema, for the duration of the bombing.

The Grand Harbour under attack by Stukas. DIGIART by JON WILKINSON

A marginal lifting of the cloud saw a formation of Ju87s swoop on the docks on the 13 January, attacking before any Hurricanes could be scrambled, but none of their 1,000kg bombs found the mark. However, the defenders knew that they weren't going to be able to rely on the weather for much longer and, if anything, the work became even more frantic as shifts worked around the clock to patch up the carrier. Preparations for the expected onslaught were also in hand at Hal Far aerodrome, where the *Illustrious'* surviving Fulmars had landed.

Grand Harbour's box barrage, now under the command of Brigadier Sadler who had masterminded the AA defences in Dover, was to be the lynchpin of the defence of the harbour and airfields, but the Hurricanes and surviving Gladiator and Fulmars would also have to play their part, the general plan being that the aircraft would pick off the German and Italian aircraft after they'd encountered the ground defences. The Fulmars were hardly designed for a battle over land, however, and the flight engineers had to be pretty inventive to enable them to fight, including 'borrowing' wing mirrors off station vehicles so that pilots, flying without their usual observers, could see what was behind them!

Thursday 16 January was a bright, sunny day and, at around 2pm, the radar at Dingli passed on the information that the defenders had been dreading, two large formations of aircraft were approaching Malta from the north. The sirens wailed and frantic shouts could be heard across the flight deck of *Illustrious* as repair crews tried to alert their colleagues working within the hull of the aircraft carrier. Escorted by Bf110s, seventeen Ju87s dipped their noses and dropped out of the sky towards Parlatorio Wharf, but the scream of their engines was drowned as the guns on the ground opened up, the Bofors being joined by the thousand-pounders based atop Rinella, St Elmo and Fort St Angelo.

Several of the Stukas didn't emerge from that first dive but the initial attack failed to seriously damage the *Illustrious*, only one bomb causing minor damage to her superstructure. However, HMS *Perth*, a destroyer left behind as added protection, was damaged below her waterline by a near-miss and the MV *Essex*, which was still having its cargo unloaded, took a direct hit. An explosion in its engine room killed fifteen crew men and five of the Maltese stevedores on board, though the carnage would have been much greater had the remaining ammunition in her holds exploded. Some estimate that large areas of the Three Cities and the *Illustrious* would have been vaporised in the resulting maelstrom.

War damage still in evidence in the streets of Vittoriosa.

The residents of Cospicua, Senglea and Vittoriosa were also being hit hard, as was Valletta across the harbour. A stricken Stuka released its bombs early as it came in from the north, demolishing a tall block of flats in what was Old Mint Street, killing five civilians. Evidence of splinter damage and repairs is still evident to this day in the area along Triq San Nikola and Triq San Dominku, downhill from the Barrakka Gardens.

Further waves of Ju87s then attacked, supported by MC200s and CR42s. Most homed in on the *Illustrious* but several over flew the carrier and dive-bombed Hal Far further south, hitting hangars and destroying three Swordfish on the ground. Luqa was also targeted, the main runway taking several hits and a Wellington bursting into flames with another suffering extensive damage, but it was the people of Senglea and Vittoriosa who suffered the most. With the *Illustrious* pretty well protected in the lee of Corrodino Heights and the

Ju 87s over the Meditteranean.

hills of Senglea, the residential areas took the brunt of the bombardment. Three hundred homes in adjacent Senglea and Cospicua were destroyed, killing fifty-three civilians, and bombs falling in Dockyard and French Creeks caused mini tidal waves along the shore-line. Rescuers faced rubble up to ten feet high as they searched for survivors in the choking dust storms that had been created and it was small consolation that the Luftwaffe had lost ten of their aircraft compared to no losses among the small number of combatant fighters from Malta. Neighbouring Vittoriosa had also been hit hard.

Outside the dock gates, the ancient auberges of the Knights of Malta, built to withstand cannon balls, hadn't fared so well against 1,000kg bombs, while the old hospital and barracks had also suffered extensive damage, but the real tragedy occurred in the crypt of the Convental Parish Church of San Lawrenzi (St Lawrence).

The church took a direct hit and forty people sheltering in its bowels died as the building collapsed on top of them, despite the efforts of ARP wardens, demolition squads and off-duty servicemen who all rushed to the scene. An impromptu first-aid post was even set up by the chief medical officer of the Cottonera Centre on the marina at Senglea to deal with casualties but events still led to a scathing editorial in the following day's *Times of Malta*, which blamed the terrible death toll on the slow reaction time of the authorities. The grim task of recovering the bodies was delegated to the Royal Engineers, King's Own Malta Regiment and the Royal Malta Artillery.

The following day saw only a light raid mounted as both sides licked their wounds, but it was to prove costly for the badly out-gunned Fulmars. Destroying only two Ju87s, two of the seaplanes failed to return to base, though Lieutenant Robert Henley and his observer were to have a lucky escape after ditching in the sea in Marsaxlokk Bay off Kalafrana. Maltese

Sapper Spiro Zammit of the Royal Engineers, who was acting as AA gunner, saw their aircraft go down and immediately jumped into the water, swimming out to where Henley and his navigator were struggling to stay afloat. Zammit held navigator Rush (a non-swimmer) above the waves until the rescue launch reached them, for which the sapper received the British Empire Medal.

The raiders were to return in numbers on Saturday 18 January, however, this time targeting Hal Far and Luqa in an attempt to nullify Malta's air defences once and for all. A formation of fifty-one Ju87s escorted by Bf110s and MC200s were met by a nine-strong combination of Hurricanes and Fulmars. The airfields again took several hits, as did the southerly town of Birzebugga, where many of the RAF personnel had their quarters, but the locals there took solace in the fact that their magnificent parish church had escaped the bombing largely intact and, for some reason, the Axis forces never seemed to consider attacking the chemical works outside the town

Bombs can be seen bursting around HMS *Illustrious*.

which could have caused massive damage had it exploded, though German policy was apparently to keep similar facilities intact so they could be utilised at a later date.

Work, meanwhile, was still progressing on board the *Illustrious*. The numbers among repair crews were kept to a minimum so that they could be evacuated to the underground dockside shelters at a moment's notice. But Chief Engineer Lieutenant Commander 'Pincher' Martin and his men, dressed only in what clothes were worth salvaging from the *Illustrious*' decimated cabins, were working tirelessly to restore her steering gear to full working order, though their toils suffered a setback when another near-miss (a bomb exploding under her hull on the bottom of Dockyard Creek) caused further damage.

Hitler personally forwarded an order to General Geisler, "Illustrious Mussen Sinken!" (The *Illustrious* Must Be Sunk!) but Malta's Dockyards were in no mood to be defeated now. Despite another massive raid on Sunday 19th, the defenders were winning the battle.

The Germans lost ten Stukas, while four of the escorting MC200s were

The dockyards alongside Fort St Angelo still carry battle scars.

shot out of the sky and the barrage laid down saw to it that there were no further hits on the *Illustrious*, though again the neighbouring towns suffered with Vittoriosa's famous clock tower incurring structural damage as well as quayside properties beneath Fort St Angelo, many of which have never been rebuilt. The Church of The Annunciation was another landmark to have its appearance altered forever when the adjoining nunnery was destroyed by what onlookers described as a 'glider bomb' and subsequent heavy rains were eventually to bring down its domed roof and transept.

Vittoriosa's clock tower was severly damaged.

But Malta had stood up to everything the *Luftwaffe* could throw at them and, six days after she'd limped into port; the *Illustrious* set sail under cover of darkness for Alexandria.

Governor Sir William Dobbie was hosting a session of the Council of Malta in the Governor's Palace in Valletta when one of his aides drew back the blackout curtain and said: 'She's off and safe'. Still covered in repair rigging, ropes and even fishing nets, she was able to make more than twenty knots en route to a major refit at the then still neutral Norfolk naval base in West Virginia, USA, via the Suez Canal and the Pacific.

The *Illustrious* was replaced by the HMS *Formidable*,

another armour-decked carrier, but the *Illustrious* was back in the Mediterranean again, following her refit, assisting in the Allied invasion of Sicily in 1943 and was also involved in the invasion of Okinawa in 1945 before seeing out her days as a training ship. Her original bell is on display in the National War Museum in Fort St Elmo.

The War Cabinet in London sent a message of thanks to Dobbie to which he replied: 'By God's help, Malta will not weaken.' It's people, however, were to have that belief tested in the months ahead.

Luftwaffe onslaught

What had been made clear by the concentrated bombing raids on *Illustrious* was that the civilian population of the Three Cities could not continue sustaining losses on the scale it had so far suffered without a serious decline in morale. So it was decided to organise an evacuation of all non-essential personnel to the countryside. Units of the Royal West Kents, the Dorsets and the Devons were tasked in commandeering the necessary transport and, though not on the scale of the trek inland in June of the previous year, almost nine thousand were bussed away from the coast.

Already overcrowded villages struggled to cope with the new influx, however, with many homeowners reluctant to adhere to the emergency law which stated those deemed to be using less than 25% of their living space must make a room available for a family of refugees. After all, who wanted to share their house with strangers? By March 1941, many were still sleeping in schools and on pews in churches, with communal kitchens, funded by the Help the Homeless Committee and Malta Relief Fund once again providing a basic diet.

Despite her problems, the War Cabinet in London was determined that

British submarine entering harbour.

Resupplying at Manoel Island submarine base.

Malta should carry on her role as a base for attacking Axis shipping in the Mediterranean, however, and U-class submarine HMS *Upholder* was to play a leading role. Stationed on the north side of Manoel Island, now home to a thriving luxury boat-building yard, the island, which is linked to land by a permanent causeway, divides Sliema Creek from Marsamxett Harbour and is best seen from one of the many harbour cruises that depart from Sliema throughout the year. It also has a long tradition of industry. Sliema Creek's deep-water channel provided ready access to Grand Harbour's entrance for the submarines, but its clear waters could also be the submariners' worst enemy.

Lieutenant-Commander Malcolm D Wankyln.

Upholder, under the commander of Lieutenant-Commander Malcolm D. Wankyln, was to become the most decorated submariner of World War II. After an undistinguished start to her service life and an almost-fatal misrecognition of sister ship *Truant*, she was to complete twenty-four patrols sinking 119,000 tons of Axis shipping and winning the Victoria Cross for Wanklyn following a successful attack on the troopship Conte Rosse. Wanklyn managed to press home an attack despite the loss of his Asdic set in a previous engagement. The Vickers-built U-Class, most of which saw service with the Second Flotilla based in Malta, was to prove particularly effective against U-boats, sinking eight in the Mediterranean alone. The boat was armed with four 21-inch stern tubes, with three .303 machine guns supporting a three-inch gun forward of the conning tower. With no hatch for the gun crew, that conning tower could become extremely crowded prior to surface action, however, and emergency dives were also next to impossible without leaving crew members on the hull.

Sadly, this led to a high mortality rate among U-class submariners and the *Upholder* and her skipper were lost in April 1942, prompting the Admiralty to take the unusual step of issuing a special statement:

> *The ship and her company are gone, but the example and the inspiration remain.*

February 1941 was to bring some relief with half of the *Fliegerkorps X* being moved to North Africa from Sicily to provide air cover for Rommel's beleaguered Afrika Corps. Yet the raids continued, with Ju88s and their Messerschmitt Bf109E escorts risking the Grand Harbour barrage to attack Ta'Qali, Luqa and Hal Far. *Hope*, one of the two remaining Gladiators, had her mid-section totally destroyed by one such raid on Hal Far as the Luftwaffe began to favour more night raids and the introduction of the BF109E also put the Mark 1 Hurricanes at a serious disadvantage.

With the BF109E, or Me109E, the first attempt was made at turning the legendary Battle of Britain German fighter into a fighter-bomber. They

Me109E with a 550 lb bomb slung underneath.

could carry a 50kg bomb under each wing yet were still nimble enough to engage the Hurricanes with their wing-mounted cannons and nose-mounted machine guns. Instead of the towns surrounding the dockyards, now it was the villages in close proximity to the airfield that were suffering serious damage.

Luqa village, in particular, was badly hit. The Church of St Andrew was pock-marked by shrapnel and bullets but somehow mostly left standing as the rest of the village square was flattened around it while St Bartholomew's leper hospital, which adjoined the old people's hospital of St Vincent de Paul, was partly destroyed when a stricken Stuka crash-landed in its gardens. That same night 14-year-old Carmela Vella was killed while sheltering in an allotment hut close to Boschetto.

Luqa village under attack.

Parachute mines were also deployed at the entrance to Grand Harbour, though many missed their target and floated into streets in Valletta and Vittoriosa, causing further damage to residential areas including the almost total destruction of the Government Elementary School in Merchants Street, next to Fort St Elmo and the famous Chapel of Bones beneath the Nibbia Chapel.

Church of St Andrew.

The Chapel of Bones, reputedly decorated with the skeletons of those who had died in the Great Siege of 1565, had been something of a tourist attraction pre-war, but it failed to survive the blast of a parachute mine and had to be completely demolished. Malta's Electoral office stands on the site today. Then there was the temptation of utilising the parachute silk. As in Britain, silk was a rare commodity and many were prepared to risk life and limb to get their hands on the material, which commanded a high price on the black market.

Chapel of Bones beneath the Nibbia Chapel had to be demolished.

The offensive wasn't one-sided, however, with Swordfish of Squadron 830 of the Fleet Air Arm sowing mines in and around the harbour at Tripoli to further hamper Italian efforts to supply the *Afrika Korps*. This was to have a tragic aftermath, though, when an exploding torpedo killed several RAF armourers and a civilian as they attempted to re-arm a Swordfish for another sortie.

Elsewhere, Hitler's planned invasion of the Soviet Union (Operation Barbarossa) was occupying most of the German hierarchy, but the Führer

Without Malta, the Axis will end by losing control of North Africa.

General Erwin Rommel

was also keen to keep an eye on his Italian allies, being particularly anxious that they adopt a more positive role in the Mediterranean with German resources likely to be at full stretch in the months ahead.

To this end, a conference was arranged in the town of Merano, on the Austro-German border, for the *Kriegsmarine* and the *Regia Aeronautica* to determine their policy regarding Malta and the Greek islands.

Generaloberst Jeschonek, chief of staff of the *Luftwaffe*, had already convinced Hitler that Malta could be nullified as an offensive base of operations by a concerted bombing campaign, and the *Wehrmacht's General* Jodl had commissioned a study as to the viability of an airborne invasion of Malta. These plans were put on hold while the new Eastern Front was established, however, with the dry-stone walls that still criss-cross Malta to this day thought likely to be a major impediment to a glider-borne or parachute assault.

'Operation Hercules' was on the back-burner for now, but the 'softening-up' of Malta's defences was to be stepped up another notch with Commander-in-chief of the *Kriegsmarine, Grand Admiral* Erich Raeder stating on the importance of Malta:

In German or Italian hands it would provide an important relief on Italian-African convoys, making the Italian naval forces, now tied up with convoy duties, available for more direct operational commitments.

Grand Admiral Erich Raeder

Chapter Six

MAC, MINES AND THE MOOR

DESPITE ILLUSTRIOUS' DEPARTURE, the bombing of Grand Harbour and Malta's airfields carried on unabated throughout February and March 1941 and collateral damage was on the increase in other areas that had previously escaped the carnage.

On the night of 13 February 1941, the AA defences at Fort Ricasoli and Fort Rinella, which still houses an Armstrong 100-ton gun billed as 'The World's Largest Cannon', came under attack, while the General Hospital at Mtarfa was struck, resulting in the deaths of Privates Scott and McGill of the Devonshires and King's Own Malta Regiment respectively. Victory Street, along with Sciberras and Senglea Wharf, suffered particularly badly, with extensive damage to several premises. Four people, including teenager Rosario Spagnol, died when they were crushed by falling debris and 10 others required hospital treatment. Buildings were also flattened in nearby St Angelo Street, Two Gates Street and Point Street, though residents who had chosen to remain in their homes were quick to adapt the cleared areas to their own advantage, stringing washing line among the rubble to air clothes that had become ingrained with post-raid dust.

Military targets were also struck with the regimental headquarters of the 12th Field Regiment (fortunately empty at the time) being totally destroyed in a raid on Luqa and the Royal Artillery taking punishment at St Clement's Bastion in Vittoriosa. The torpedo depot at Msida was another

The 100-ton gun at Fort Rinella.

target, while a Sunderland flying boat was set alight in St Paul's Bay, though the island's defences were to be boosted by the arrival of an additional AA battery from Alexandria and further anti-aircraft positions were established at St Julian's, Dragut Point and on Gozo.

Though there had been little indication that Malta's sister island was a target for invasion, a small number of infantrymen were sent to bolster the local militia. Gozo was also the setting for one of the more bizarre moments of the war when a lone Ju87 began 'buzzing' the Gozo ferry mid-channel. Unopposed, the pilot circled the ferry until it docked in Mgarr harbour (72) and then waited until all of its passengers and crew had disembarked and scurried away from the quayside before sinking the vessel with cannon-fire. That was a rare act of compassion between the two forces, however, and the fact that there were now more guns defending Grand Harbour than the whole of London still didn't stop the *Luftwaffe* from continuing their offensive!

As was the case with Lieutenant Commander Wanklyn and the *Upholder*, some were destined to etch their name in Malta's military folklore at this time. One such was Flight Lieutenant J.A.F. MacLachlan. A Hurricane pilot and a survivor of ill-fated Operation White the previous November, MacLachlan had already earned the DFC by the time he was twenty-one and was highly regarded among the men of 261 Squadron based at Ta'Qali. But his luck ran out on the morning of 16 February when six Bf109Es attacked his flight. MacLachlan's aircraft was badly shot up and he was forced to bail out, having suffered wounds to his shoulder and left arm. He was eventually ferried to Mtarfa Hospital where, on a mixture of whisky and morphine, he was patched up and transferred to a general

Mtarfa Hospital.

ward. Unfortunately, surgeons eventually had to amputate his mangled arm but MacLachlan refused to be deterred by his disability, learning to fly with an artificial arm and he was flying sorties over Western Europe again in his beloved Hurricane by 1943. 'One-Armed Mac', as he affectionately became known, was to earn promotion to the rank of Squadron Leader and add a DSO to his DFC before he was shot down again over France in July 1943. He sadly died of his injuries in a POW camp that summer.

It's difficult to imagine nowadays as you travel around this holiday island, but even the Maltese beaches in 1941 could be deadly places. Thousands of mines had been sown by the British in the Western Mediterranean, in lines extending from Sardinia to Tunisia and from the heel of Italy via Sicily to Libya, with the Axis countries laying their ordnance, both acoustic and magnetic, around Malta and Gozo to trap the convoys. Inevitably in the traditionally bad weather between January and March, many of these mines were cut adrift by rough seas and washed ashore. Gozo, in particular, with its sheltered bays became very vulnerable and special squads had to be detailed in places such as Mgarr, Xlendi and Ramla Bay to ensure no harm came to the local population.

The mines set by the Germans and Italians were taking their toll on shipping arriving at the entrance to Grand Harbour as well. HMS *Abingdon* and HMS *Fermoy* comprised Malta's minesweeping force but they weren't equipped to deal with the new parachute mines, so the Royal Navy were forced to turn to the converted drifter HMS *Ploughboy*, which had been fitted with a magnetic sweep, to keep shipping on the move. *Ploughboy* couldn't hope to neutralise every mine, however, and two

Mine clearing on Gozo.

HMS *Fermoy.*

sailors died when a boat bound for Gozo was struck. The former fishing boat also suffered the loss of two of its own crew 10 March when, escorting the submarine *Regent* back to base on Manoel Island, she detonated a mine in Marsamxett and, listing dangerously, had to be beached while repairs were carried out. But the most devastating blow to the Maltese came on 8 April. The entrance to Grand Harbour was protected by a series of boom nets, one of which stretched from a place known locally as Taht iz-Ziemel near St Elmo Point to Ricasoli Point. This series of ropes and chains, especially made in Scotland, supported steel nets (made locally) and were secured to the rock by giant hawsers. They required constant maintenance because of the wear and tear involved in winching them open and closed. Hollow metal

Maltese women were often employed in the assembly and repair of anti-submarine booms.

spheres and old oil drums, used as floats, were also susceptible to damage from falling bombs and it was the job of the crew of the MV *Moor* to ensure all these components were in working order 24 hours a day.

Every vessel that plied its trade in and around Grand Harbour was supplied with charts that highlighted the 'no-go' areas but, for some reason on that fateful day, possibly because it was the end of a long shift, the coxswain of the *Moor*, Guzeppi Muzelli, decided to take a short cut across from the harbour entrance to the dockyards. The boat struck a magnetic mine it had disturbed on the seabed and sank almost immediately. Of the twenty-nine Maltese crew on board, only diver Anthony Mercieca was rescued.

He described his ordeal thus:

> *An explosion struck the vessel and I was flung to the floor. I found the ship sinking beneath me and a lot of wreckage around me. Some planks pinned me down. I somehow got my head free and rose to the surface. But again I found myself being twirled around by the vortex created by the sinking ship.*

Mercieca was plucked out of the sea by sister ship the *Westgate*, the only injury he suffered being a gash on his chin. But, of his colleagues, only one more body was found on the surface, though Bomb Disposal Officer Commander Kenneth Campbell had a lucky escape. A regular crew member of the *Moor*, he'd just been put ashore on the Ricasoli breakwater to assess the condition of one of the boom's mountings and could only watch in horror as his shipmates perished.

There's a marble plaque situated in Upper Barrakka Gardens commemorating the sacrifice made by the crew of the Moor, and they weren't the only ones to meet their fate in this fashion. In May of that year, destroyer HMS *Jersey* was to hit a mine and sink, blocking the harbour entrance. Thirty-four of her crew didn't survive.

SUPPLY AND DEMAND

On 12 February, compulsory conscription of all qualified able-bodied men became law in Malta with those aged between twenty-one and twenty-five required to register for military service in the armed forces with others asked to volunteer for local regiments. This was an alien step for many Maltese men who were unaccustomed to sharing rooms with anyone but their family and had never before encountered the level of discipline demanded by the British. Some, especially those who lived in outlying villages, didn't even wear shoes so to be kitted out with hobnail boots also came as a culture shock. Many had never worn a tie, or seen a rifle yet, within a matter of weeks, most of the new recruits could strip down and re-assemble a Bren gun in the dark and turned out on parade with the brass gleaming on their uniforms and caps. 'A dirty soldier means a dirty rifle, a dirty rifle means a dead soldier.' was one of the military sayings of the day. Conscription was a major step for Malta, but it was a step that had been a long time in planning.

King's Own Malta Regiment.

Ever since the Abyssinia crisis of 1935, there had been a gradual mobilisation of the island's available manpower with a programme in place to expand the Maltese regiments. In 1938, in response to Italian and German expansionism, the Royal Malta Artillery had been split into two with its ranks swelled from 500 to almost 1500 men, many trained in the operation of AA equipment at Fort Ricasoli, which was to be established as the island's recruit training depot.

The King's Own Malta Regiment, a part-time unit, also recruited enough volunteers to form two extra battalions and was moved to a new base at Sterling Barracks in Fort Campbell behind the Selmun Palace above Mellieha Bay, in the north of the island, away from the traditional regimental head-quarters at Pembroke. The regiment was to play a key role in the guarding of airfields and manning pill-boxes and checkpoints in case of invasion, often with Bren-gun carriers or in light-armoured vehicles like the Matilda.

Pembroke Barracks in Fort Campbell.

When hostilities began, there was also plenty of work for the mechanics, drivers and despatch riders of the Malta Auxiliary Corps, who were attached to the British

British Matilda tank on display.

regiments on the islands, the Devons, Dorsets, Irish Fusiliers and West Kents. The Corps also supplied the majority of field medics and stretcher-bearers.

Another notable addition to the defences was the amalgamation of the 10th, 22nd and 30th AA battery, the famous Dockyard Battery, with the 15th Battery. The latter was made up entirely of conscripts but more than 5000 had volunteered when the call had first gone out for workers to divide their time between the dockyard and its defence. There were also two Coast Regiments responsible for guarding the shoreline against small-scale assault. They would also have been the first line of defence in the event of a sea-borne invasion and were to enjoy their finest hour in July 1941, more of which later. The fact that conscription was eventually introduced shouldn't detract from the fact, however, that 1,400 Maltese had already volunteered for service in the Royal Navy, the majority in warships.

Though a four-ship convoy had got through in the early months of 1941, supplies were beginning to run out in the Maltese islands and April saw the beginning of wholesale rationing, though it was probably a measure of Britain's relative ignorance of the situation that Churchill's government had still inquired if Malta would be exporting its usual quota of potatoes to the UK!

Rubble surrounds the former Food Distribution Centre.

A Food Distribution Centre was set up in Old Bakery Street, Valletta, where Commerce Control Officers issued stock to the 10 regions designated under emergency laws, though this had to be temporarily moved in early 1942 when much of the area was flattened in a raid.

Wholesalers were only allowed to sell to specified retailers who, in turn, had a list of families to whom they could sell supplies. Individuals were not allowed to buy from more than one shop and specific goods like sugar, matches, soap and coffee had restrictions placed upon them. Permits were also needed to stock milk, lard, margarine, tea and rice, though infants and the infirm were allocated a generous allowance of tinned milk and the NAAFI maintained its own cache for servicemen, though 'bully beef' often appeared on the menu more often than many would have liked!

But the biggest problem was the distribution of kerosene, which was widely used for cooking, heating and light. Carts selling the fuel were escorted by police officers to prevent civilians getting more than the stipulated amount. Despite assurances by the Lieutenant Governor's office that the price would not increase whatever the circumstances, householders began hording the fuel in increasing amounts causing a shortage of its own. It prompted an official statement that read;

> *The time for laying in private reserves of kerosene is now over. The quantities now supplied to cart men are to meet ordinary immediate requirements and the public must co-operate in an unselfish spirit and limit their purchases accordingly.*
>
> (Joseph Micallef, *When Malta Stood Alone*)

The actual distribution of kerosene was in the hands of the Deputy Controller of Mineral Oils (in actuality the local manager of the Shell Oil company), who employed the drivers of the horse-drawn tank-carts that distributed up to a gallon of the fuel to each family every week. It wasn't a perfect system and occasionally, whether because of bombing raids or 'disappearances' to the black market, some went without but, by and large, most people got their fair share of the dwindling supply.

Supplies on their way to the beleaguered island.

Chapter Seven

BACKS TO THE WALL

BETWEEN November 1940 and March 1941, the Axis forces had lost more than 100,000 tonnes of shipping in the Mediterranean. But spring had seen the Italians begin to have more success with their convoys to Tripoli, ships steering a wider route to take them clear of Malta and largely out of range of its offensive forces. The supplies they carried helped the *Africa Korps* take Benghazi, but the RAF and Fleet Air Arm never gave up their search for targets, even though increased raids on Luqa had led to the withdrawal of the Wellington bombers.

There was some good news for the Allies; the Italians were incurring heavy losses in the Battle of Cape Matapan. Royal Navy's Force K sank three cruisers and two destroyers and the subsequent short-term absence of Italian vessels in the area prompted the Royal Navy to make another attempt to replenish Malta's Hurricane numbers. Flanked by cruisers HMS *Renown* and HMS *Sheffield* and five destroyers, the aircraft carrier HMS *Ark Royal* took delivery of twelve Mark II Hurricanes via the *Argus* at Gibraltar. The aircraft arrived safely on the island and Operation Winch was deemed an unqualified success, but the situation on Malta continued to deteriorate.

For the first time ever across the islands, the church bells sounded on a

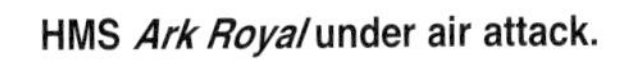

HMS *Ark Royal* under air attack.

British cruisers HMS *Sheffield* (above) and HMS *Renown* (below), along with five destroyers, escorted HMS *Ark Royal* into Malta's Grand Harbour to deliver twelve Hurricane fighter planes.

Good Friday; however they weren't calling the faithful to prayer they were sounding the all clear after yet another heavy raid. Having left briefly to assist in the invasion of Greece and Yugoslavia, the Luftwaffe had returned in force and the Hurricane pilots and ground crew were again at full stretch. Good Friday saw the loss of five of the Hurricanes in a prolonged sequence of dogfights that lasted well into the night.

Precious machines in the defence of the islands – the Hawker Hurricane.

Pilot Officer Hamish Hamilton even took to the air wearing his flying tunic over his pyjamas. He did shoot down a Stuka but RAF victories came at a cost. A stricken Ju87 crashing into a farmhouse at Sqaq ta' Lanzar near Maghtab, killing youngster Rosaria Mifsud, while another four civilians died as bombs were dropped on residential areas near Ta'Qali and at Siggiewi.

The revered Oratorio Sacre Famiglia in Siggiewi was destroyed and the New Street and St Nicholas Street areas also suffered severe damage. Bombs rained down on the Hospital For Mental Diseases at Attard as well. It appears the Luftwaffe had been mis-informed as to the use of the hospital buildings for it became a target for concerted attacks over the next few days with the female dormitory taking a direct hit on the night of 14 April, killing two patients and injuring twelve others. Some of those injured had only been moved to Attard at the beginning of the year when the St Vincent de Paul Hospital had been damaged in a raid. The bombing had taken out telephone and power lines, but the staff at the hospital refused to allow the darkness or the crumbling masonry to deter their rescue attempts and they somehow managed to get all the wounded, many bed-ridden or invalids, to Bujega Hospital in Birkikara, despite the patients' terrified and confused state.

Being a nation of devout Roman Catholics, the Maltese regard Easter Sunday as a day of national celebration, but 1941 was to prove a year the islanders would not remember with any fondness. Dawn brought the 500th alert since the commencement of hostilities and the loss of two more Hurricanes. Malta's defenders had now accounted for more than 130 Axis aircraft with a further 44 unconfirmed losses, but the death toll among civilians had risen to 270.

The following days brought further attacks on Mtarfa military hospital, with the isolation ward taking a direct hit. Nearby Mdina was also attacked. The walled city, across the valley floor from Mtarfa, had no military importance and had escaped relatively lightly previously but bombs struck several homes on April 14th, including a recently built house in the Strada Santa Sofia, which had its staircase and most of its lower floor

Dwellings and public buildings were gradually being reduced to piles of rubble.

destroyed. The dazed occupants somehow survived, and were led to safety the following morning by way of an upstairs balcony and a ladder.

The heavy bombing was sapping morale and was also beginning to affect the island's infrastructure, with authorities struggling to maintain water supplies in the most severely damaged areas in the Three Cities, Floriana and Valletta. Valletta had been well served by its underground reservoirs over the years, but the ability to deliver water to homes inside and beyond the city walls was slowly being eradicated by the Luftwaffe. During April alone, there had been 48 pipe bursts in the capital and motor-driven water tankers had to be drafted in to ensure drinking water could be distributed by volunteers armed with buckets

In Vittoriosa, the tank in St Clemence Parade Ground (situated on the opposite side of the road to the Malta At War Museum), which supplied the Three Cities, received a direct hit as did the reserve tank at St James Cavalier in Valletta's Great Ditch, though the latter was able to function after emergency repairs. Often, a surface pipe system had to be laid because debris in the streets made it impossible to access underground

Queueing for water.

Three escorts lead the *Breconshire* safely into harbour.

pipes though these, of course, were more vulnerable to bomb damage and were never intended as anything more than temporary measures.

By June 1941, the island's reserves of fresh water had shrunk by almost a third and, with the hot summer months ahead, there were anxious times in store for the Civil Administration despite the siege of Grand Harbour having been lifted by the arrival of the armed tanker *Breconshire* and her naval escort from Alexandria, followed by a seven-ship convoy from the Egyptian port some three weeks later.

The Germans were now in Athens, and Crete had fallen to an airborne invasion that had both surprised and overwhelmed the British Forces who had anticipated a beach assault – would Malta be next.

Life goes on

Despite the incessant bombing and the ever-increasing fear of invasion, the people of Malta still had to get to work and their children had to get to school. Petrol rationing meant that the bus timetable was severely restricted but those living around Grand Harbour and its environs had others options.

The people of the Three Cities and Sliema could commute on the coal-fired lighters of the National Steam Ferry Boat Company. Operated by a two-man crew these tiny steamers, flying the company's traditional orange and blue pennant, ploughed across the water from dawn to dusk and were a lifeline to many families who had no other means of transport. The traditional dghajsa could also carry up to 10 people at a time, though potential passengers were often reluctant to take the risk of being caught in open water on a rowing boat in the middle of an air-raid and the fumes given off by oil spills in the harbour were known to make non-sailors nauseous (the smell was masked by the smoke on the steam ferry).

Considering how close Sliema was to Valletta, the Germans and Italians had largely left the town alone. No warships were berthed in Sliema Creek and Marsamxett Harbour had remained empty since the start of the war.

This had led to many residents having a relaxed view about the bombing raids, but that attitude was changed forever on the 10 March.

The *Plumleaf* became a target for the *Luftwaffe*

The *Plumleaf*, a battered and rusting oil tanker attached to the Royal Navy reserve fleet, was only ever moved from her permanent home at Ta' Xbiex Point to scrape barnacles from her hull. But the decision was taken to move her into Sliema Creek and tie her up between two buoys immediately opposite the Nazarene Church. Sure enough, this potential target was soon spotted by a flight of Bf109s and, just after 9.00pm, the sirens sounded warning civilians to take cover. In Sliema, however, this was the signal for the more curious to head for the nearest roof to watch the searchlights pick out the enemy aircraft and the batteries of Fort Manoel and Fort Rinella to try and bring them down – they just didn't expect the bombs to fall on their own homes.

There was mass panic as residents suddenly realised that their town was the target of the bombers, with people falling over each other in the darkness of the blackout as they sought shelter. It had long been a bone of contention that Sliema didn't have adequate underground shelters for its population, and this night that deficiency was to prove costly. St Rita Street, adjoining main coast road The Strand, suffered the worst of the damage with one side of the street almost totally demolished. Many were buried under tons of rubble and live cables left exposed by the explosions electrocuted one poor soul who was searching for his family. It was another harsh lesson that no community was safe from the bombing.

Repairing electric cables following a raid.

Elsewhere in the Mediterranean theatre, things were also going badly for the Allies. Already struggling to maintain a supply route to Malta, the Royal Navy was also now tasked with providing the rations and ammunitions needed to sustain the beleaguered defenders of Tobruk, who were surrounded on three sides by the rampant Afrika Korps. By April, Rommel had advanced to within touching distance of the Egyptian border and Britain had surrendered all the gains they had made earlier in the year.

It was time for a rallying cry from London and Churchill summoned his Chiefs of Staff to Whitehall for a detailed assessment of the situation. The Prime Minister understood that it was imperative that the German supply line through Tripoli was disrupted. Unmolested, they would be able to replenish vastly superior armoured columns via the coastal roads and smash British resistance in North Africa. Admiral Cunningham, therefore, was to be given greater resources that in turn meant a bigger RAF presence on Malta to help protect the new naval offensive that was to intercept the Axis convoys.

Admiral Cunningham.

Cunningham was well aware of the threat posed by the Ju87s and Ju88s, however, and also the perilous state of supplies in Malta, stating later;

> *It was obvious that with the lack of air cover this force could only work by night. At sea it would be at the mercy of dive-bombers. Good air reconnaissance from Malta was also essential for finding the convoys, as was the fighter defence. The dockyard was steadily been knocked to bits by enemy bombers.*

The X Flotilla

Towards the end of World War I, the Italian Navy had been at the forefront of a new form of warfare, the use of manned torpedoes, mini-submarines and divers to mine enemy ships in harbour. This specialised branch was to become known as the X Light Flotilla and had two divisions – surface and underwater – both of which had already seen action in the Mediterranean in ultimately unsuccessful attacks on Alexandria and Gibraltar, despite Italian claims to the contrary. Undeterred, the *Regia Navale* deemed that Malta's Grand Harbour was a perfect target for the surface section of their attack force and, by April 1941, detailed plans were already well advanced for the assault.

barchini, flat-bottomed speedboats.

The attack was to be pressed home by a flotilla of barchini, flat-bottomed speedboats powered by an Alfa-Romeo outboard motor that enabled the low-slung craft to reach speeds of over 30mph. The boats were steered by a pilot, who aimed the barchini at a specific target, allowing the charge contained in the bows to detonate on impact (though some could also be set off by hydrostatic pressure). Once the target had been acquired and the rudder locked, the pilot would then eject along with his backrest, which was designed to shield him from the worst of the explosive concussion as well as keep him afloat until the accompanying rescue boat could pick him up.

Reconnaissance missions took place in May and June to ascertain the exact positions of the booms and nets in Grand Harbour, project leader Commander Vittorio Moccagatta himself using the cover of air raids to also plot the position of the shore-based guns that could threaten his boats. What he didn't see was that the harbour defences had a surface radar post, and that was to prove a fatal error. The attack was planned for 28 June, but unseasonable heavy seas caused a postponement and when the green light was given two days later, engine trouble prevented the sloop *Diana*, which was to act as the barchini transporter, from leaving port.

As it was to be a night attack, X Flotilla now suffered a further delay. The moon was almost full and Moccagatta couldn't risk his men being spotted by the lookouts situated in Tigne Fort and Fort St Elmo. This delay gave Moccagatta a chance to revise his options. He also had at his disposal two-man human torpedoes, known as SLCs, which had been developed by naval engineer Major Teseo Tesei at the start of the war.

Tesei's enthusiasm for his SLCs was infectious and he convinced Moccagatta that his mini-submarines would be able

Left: Major Teseo Tesei.
Below: An Italian two-man human torpedo.

to enter Grand Harbour undetected and disable the anti-submarine nets. A route had been decided underneath the steel arch bridge that spanned a channel close to the base of Fort St Elmo, which was normally used by small coastal craft.

The plan now, therefore, was for the *Diana* to tow a motorboat, carrying two human torpedoes, to within nine miles of Malta before releasing them. She was to be accompanied by two motor-torpedo boats that carried the barchini and towed a small motorboat, from which the attack would be co-ordinated. It was intended that the barchini would be released for their final run into Grand Harbour at a point almost a mile from the harbour entrance once the SLCs had disabled the boom and anti-submarine nets.

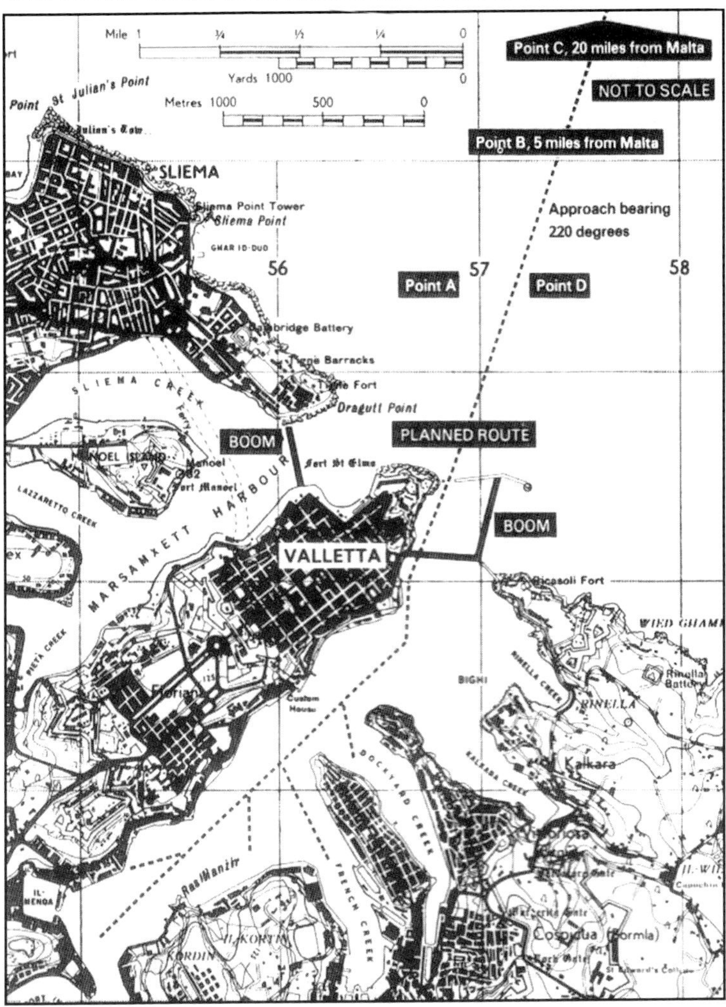

Once inside, any naval vessel was to be regarded as a target for the mines and torpedoes and the intention was for the motor-torpedo boats to also slip in amid the confusion to provide cover while the pilots of the barchini were rescued.

Calm seas, meanwhile, had returned and conditions were deemed suitable for the flotilla to set sail 26 July 1941 – but things began to go wrong almost from the outset. While in harbour, the *Diana's* towing cable fouled the propeller of one of the motor-torpedo boats and it collided with the accompanying motor boat, opening up a gash in the former's bow and meaning she had to be temporarily left behind.

The boats reached their rendezvous off Fort St Elmo on schedule but, on launching, one of the SLCs immediately developed a list towards her stern which couldn't be corrected and she had to turn back meaning Major Tesei was left alone to disable the nets. To add to his problems, the operation was now running well behind schedule. Tesei was meant to use the distraction of a *Regia Aeronautica* raid on Luqa to execute his attack, but the Major realised that he was also certainly on a suicide mission now as he would only be able to give himself a minute to get clear before the fuses on the mines exploded if he were not to compromise his comrades.

Bravely, Tesei disappeared into the darkness, unflinching in his duty. But his sacrifice was to be in vain. Unknown to the Italians, the *Diana* and her small flotilla had been picked up by Malta's radar the previous evening and the Royal Malta Artillery was on full alert, even though the defenders had no detailed knowledge of the threat they faced.

Wrecked pier below Fort St Elmo.

The air raid on Luqa began early and when an explosion was heard at 4.25am, five minutes ahead of Tesei's scheduled time of attack, the assault co-ordinator wrongly assumed that the nets had been blown and ordered the barchini to advance. The first of the human-torpedoes aimed for the steel-arch bridge that jutted out from the pier below Fort St Elmo but the boat struck the still-intact anti-submarine net and failed to explode. In the water, pilot Sottotenente Frassetto desperately tried to signal those following to change course but the second barchini was already on its run and struck the concrete pier, killing pilot Sototenente Carabelli instantly. The force of the explosion caused one half of the steel bridge to collapse into the water , effectively blocking the Italians' planned route of entry.

The explosion, of course, alerted the shore defences and searchlights immediately lit up the sky and danced across the water's surface. Sergeant Zammit of the Royal Malta Artillery was overlooking the bridge and describes what happened next;

Suddenly I saw a motor-torpedo boat heading towards the breakwater. I gave the alarm and my gun went into action just as the MTB hit the bridge and blew up. Searchlights illuminated the scene as I saw three others heading towards Grand Harbour. All guns fired at them and one was destroyed and the others disabled.

Two of the remaining barchini had slipped into the main channel but their fate was also sealed. Zammit again;

I saw them zigzagging and turning at high-speed to avoid the very heavy punishment they were taking. They were still sunk.

Crowds had now gathered on the bastions overlooking the harbour, despite the early hour. It was like a scene from one of Malta's famous saint-day fiestas as the green and red tracer shells bounced off the surface of the water and into the lightening sky like fireworks.

X Flotilla was now in full retreat but their ordeal wasn't over as Hurricanes, scrambled by radar, now arrived, strafing the motor-torpedo boats as they fled northwards. Moccagatta was one of the first to perish, before he had time to contemplate the failure of his brainchild, and the Hurricanes continued to press home their attack even though a flight of Macchi 200 was sent out from

Below: broken piers today. Hurricanes straffed the attackers.

Italian Motor Torpedo Boat.

Comiso to provide air cover for the fleeing boats. Only nine men found their way back to base, fifteen having lost their lives in the assault with eighteen taken prisoner having been picked up by British rescue launches in the vicinity of Grand Harbour. The Italians even had to suffer the indignity of having a shot-down Hurricane pilot capture one of the abandoned barchini.

There was no doubting the courage of the men of X Flotilla, but they'd been undone by their ignorance of Malta's harbour defences and dogged by equipment problems. The *Diana*, which had allegedly been built as Mussolini's private yacht, only survived another year before being sunk off Tobruk, but one of the key components of this engagement can still be seen to this day. Walk down Triq il-Mediterran towards Fort St Elmo from Upper Barrakka Gardens and look towards the harbour entrance. The bridge may have gone but the piers remain where this fateful attack floundered.

Anxious times

The fall of Crete hung over Malta as heavily as the palls of smoke that lay across Grand Harbour following a raid. But, unknown to the islanders or the British, the islands were safe from invasion for now, though a siren in the dockyards that had been short-circuited by an explosion panicked those sheltering from the bombs in Floriana. It sounded continuously for more than two hours prompting residents to flee from their underground bunkers into the barrage to ascertain if the 'invasion' had started.

Fortunately, an alert Royal Artillery officer was able to herd them back to safety before anyone was hurt.

Crete may have ultimately been a huge success for the *Luftwaffe*, who had instigated the invasion with minimal consultation with the *Wehrmacht* and the *Kriegsmarine*, but it had come at a price in the number of German casualties prompting Hitler, with the invasion of the Soviet Union at the forefront of his thinking, to reprimand General Kurt Student commander of the paratroop division, and put a ban on all similar planned undertakings in the near future. Britain, too, had suffered in Crete. A massive rescue operation had been launched to evacuate troops from the beaches but more than half the garrison were still taken prisoner, such was the speed of the German advance. More immediate to Malta, however, was the supply situation.

Operation Tiger got through to Alexandria via Gibraltar, carrying valuable tanks for the Eighth Army in Egypt as well as Hurricanes for the RAF, and Operation Substance set sail for Malta on 21 July escorted by the aircraft carrier HMS *Ark Royal*, battleship HMS *Nelson* and cruisers *Arethusa*, *Edinburgh* and *Manchester*, the convoy suffered an early setback when the troop carrier *Leinster*, carrying RAF ground crew bound for Luqa, ran aground in fog (they later reached their destination on the ships among Operation Style in August). There were also worries that the convoy's security had been compromised by an errant NAAFI request for provisions that wasn't passed through secure channels. Nevertheless, the remaining six merchantmen reached their destination on 24 July; though the *Sydney Star* limped into Grand Harbour a number of hours after the main convoy having been set upon by Italian E-boats within sight of the islands and both the *Manchester* and the destroyer HMS *Fearless* suffered damage in air raids.

The Italians had been far more reticent about sending their fleet into battle since the partial withdrawal of their German air cover and this hesitancy was also to allow a number of merchantmen that had been trapped in the harbour to escape, including the armed tanker *Breconshire*, but essential rations were still running low. Fresh imported meat was no longer available and rabbit, a favourite dish on Malta to this day, had become very scarce while the fishing fleet had obvious difficulties to overcome. The Maltese also liked to supplement their diet by snaring and shooting migratory birds along the southern cliffs but this was another potential food source that had become impractical to pursue.

With *Fliegerkorps X* now in Crete, there were some who believed the avenue between Gibraltar and Malta had become less dangerous as convoys arrived with much-needed supplies during August and September, but Operation Halberd was soon to alter this perception. As in Operation Substance, the *Ark Royal* and the *Nelson* were tasked with

Above: The Ark Royal listing to starboard after being struck by a torpedo from the *U81*, *Kapitänleutnant* Guggenberger.

Right: German propaganda had 'sunk' the *Ark Royal* on previous occasions, now at last they had something to celebrate.

„Schwerpunkt des Angriffs: Der Flugzeugträger"

Below: HMS *Barham* operating in the Mediterranean.

Bottom and inset: The *Barham* after been struck by three torpedoes from the *U331*, *Kapitänleutnant* von Tiesenhausen rolls to port before exploding killing 841 men.

Admiral Dönetz sent more U-Boats to the Mediterranean.

providing the firepower behind a shield of destroyers, but disaster struck on 27 September when a U-boat torpedoed the *Ark Royal*. Germany was determined to maintain the siege on Malta and, even though it could no longer concentrate all of its air power on the island, ten U-boats had been transferred to the Mediterranean from operations in the Atlantic and it was one of these that had attacked the *Ark Royal*. The aircraft carrier eventually rolled over. With the merchant ship *Imperial Star* also suffering irreparable damage and having to be scuttled, the Admiralty decided to call a temporary halt to Malta convoys and explore other sea born methods of getting essential supplies through.

Flying flags of convenience, the merchantmen *Empire Pelican* and *Empire Defender* tried to reach the islands via a circuitous route through coastal

Every ship which successfully ran the gauntlet gave heart to the besieged islanders.

waters but both were spotted and sunk. This caused the abandonment of a planned copycat mission and the cancellation of an attempt by the oil tanker SS *Thorshavet* to reach Malta.

The RAF continued targeting Axis convoys to Libya and its harassment of Italian bases in Sicily, but November brought further bad news with the sinking of the *Ark Royal* off Gibraltar and the torpedoing of HMS *Barham* and, in contrast to the relative optimism that had ended the previous year, Christmas 1941 saw morale at an all-time low despite the naval stores being raided to ensure the NAAFI Christmas pudding could be served with a traditional rum sauce.

A lone Italian reconnaissance plane 'hand-delivered' a Christmas card to Ta'Qali on Christmas Day, but hostilities resumed again on Boxing Day and, with the Italian *Flotilla X* learning its lessons in Malta by crippling two battleships in Alexandria harbour, only the ever-reliable *Breconshire* lifted the gloom by managing to get through to Malta with her cargo of oil.

The second Great Siege of Malta was about to enter its decisive phase.

Chapter Eight

SPITFIRES AND THE GEORGE CROSS

We must be obviously ready for drastic reduction in issues of essential commodities.

Lieutenant General Sir William Dobbie, January 1942

THERE were no celebrations on New Year's Day 1942. The *Luftwaffe* and *Regia Aeronautica* still enjoyed a massive numerical advantage over the Hurricanes, whose pilots were now becoming battle-weary due to being on constant alert. The first day of the New Year brought another early-morning raid, which battered the installations around Grand Harbour and civilian targets in Valletta and the Three Cities. There were twenty-six fatalities, with another fourteen seriously injured and the bombardment carried on through the next 36 hours into 3 January with Ta'Qali and Luqa

Hal Far suffers yet another raid.

airfields taking particularly heavy punishment.

Food was also becoming more scarce, with civilians and the cooks in the services forced to become even more inventive with what they had available. Flight Sergeant (later to become Air Marshal) Ivor Broom describes in *Malta, The Last Great Siege* by David Wragg how monotonous the standard diet had become:

> *We lived on Maconochies, which was meat and vegetables tinned, and we had it in every form and guise you can have it. The food was dull and repetitive. We had this meat and vegetables fried, stewed, in pies, we had it curried, all sorts of ways.*

But at least the servicemen were guaranteed one square meal a day. Sadly this was not the case among the Maltese, especially those still determined to see out the war in their homes along the eastern and southern coasts.

Queing was to become the norm.

The 'bread' ration had been reduced to just over ten ounces per day per adult but was of such poor quality that nobody nowadays would recognise it as the traditionally spongy Maltese bread that's served up in restaurants and street cafes. Bran and even potatoes were being added to the flour and dough which would turn the end product a very dark, almost black colour, giving it a sour taste as well as a coarse texture. It would also quickly go mouldy if not consumed.

One pint of goat's milk per family was distributed daily, but civilian kerosene supplies had almost run out and could now only be acquired with coupons, the amount decided by the size of the family.

Before the war, the word 'queue' hadn't existed in the Maltese language, but now everyone knew its meaning. Any amount of queuing couldn't get the items that weren't available, however, and this applied in particular to new clothes and shoes. So much so that, by the beginning of 1942, people had resorted to scouring bombed-out buildings in search of usable garments and footwear.

Charles B Grech in *Raiders Passed* describes how he struck lucky on one occasion as a child in Sliema:

> *I was lucky enough to find a pair of shoes similar to those my father wore when he was a kid. I tried to clean off the caked dust that seemed glued to*

them but, of course, no shoe polish was available. I went into the kitchen, got some lard and some soot, mixed them on the fire and when the mixture had cooled down again, I used it as shoe polish. Alas, after I had taken a few steps in my "new" shoes I felt them pressing on my feet like a clamp, because they were the wrong size after all!

Most people weren't as lucky as Grech and had to make do with homemade sandals made of either wood and sackcloth or rope tied around discarded pieces of car tyre rubber.

Foraging in rubbish bins was becoming commonplace, especially around Valletta and the Three Cities, and even the corab trees that grew on the slopes around St Julian's were being stripped for their seeds. With the potato crop almost certain to fail due to a lack of fertilizer, the authorities knew they had to act to prevent possible outbreaks of dysentery from unsafe food sources so they set up what were to become known as 'Victory Kitchens', initially in the most deprived areas, to ensure that the populace would be guarantee one warm meal a day without the risk of food poisoning.

Based on the Community Kitchens which had proved successful earlier in the siege, the Victory Kitchens charged sixpence a day for a meal with the production of a ration book and commonly served up goat stew, vegetable soup (minestra), herrings, sardines, bulbiliata (a tomato and egg powder concoction) and beans or macaroni, dependent on what was available from centrally located stores on a particular day. 'Veal' was served as an occasional treat, though this was actually, more often than not, horsemeat and the poor animals slaughtered were so undernourished their flesh was only just edible.

Legislation was also passed preventing people from collecting wood from demolished buildings so that the kitchens' ovens and bakeries could cut down on their use of kerosene as a fuel, and this was extended to include the balconies of properties still standing which occasionally 'disappeared' during the night or in the aftermath of a raid.

Malta's 223 listed bakeries had long since been banned from producing the sour cream cakes and pastries that are so popular in Malta today, but bread was a staple part of the wartime diet and its production was to be protected at all cost, even though all the people had to spread on it was lard as butter and margarine had long since disappeared from the shelves.

By June 1942, the monthly rations for a family of five had been reduced to two and a half pounds of sugar, half a pound of cheese, a quarter pound of tea, a pound of lard, half a pound of coffee, four tins of corned beef, four tins of fish, four pints of oil and three bars of soap. By the end of the summer, the numbers using the Victory Kitchens had risen from 7,000 in February to more than 60,000 and to make matters worse, the Sarsons brewery had been forced to close down with its grain stocks exhausted.

Cases of scabies were also on the rise due to the poor diet and lice infestations were becoming common as hygiene suffered through lack of adequate washing facilities. British servicemen weren't immune either. A stomach bug known as 'Malta Dog' affected virtually everyone who was posted to the island at some stage and, though it passed through the system fairly quickly, was bad enough to confine even the most hardy of individuals to barracks for 48 hours. It was said a chalk and opium mixture washed down with port and brandy would alleviate the symptoms, but that was probably wishful thinking on behalf of the afflicted!

Fuel shortages meant that there was little hot water for bathing so residents resorted to leaving a tin bath full of cold water on the flat roof during the day, hoping the sun would warm it by evening. Of course, with raids around the clock, this also meant that the bath was usually full of dust by the time someone came to use it and there were also privacy issues with taking a bath in full view of the entire neighbourhood.

Any semblance of normal life was gradually grinding to a halt with even the buses now only able to operate a reduced service during peak times in the most populated areas. Those living in outlying villages had to walk or hitch a lift on a passing horse and cart as servicemen were now commandeering bicycles.

Militarily, however, progress was being made, particularly in the protection of Malta's aerial defence force. The prolonged attacks on the airfields and subsequent loss of aircraft on the ground had prompted Air

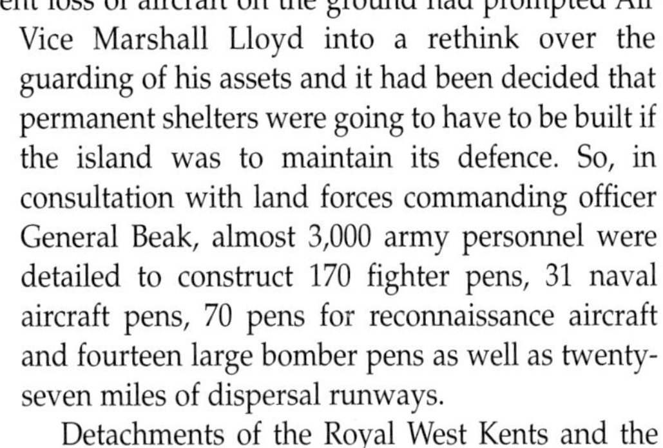

Vice Marshall Lloyd into a rethink over the guarding of his assets and it had been decided that permanent shelters were going to have to be built if the island was to maintain its defence. So, in consultation with land forces commanding officer General Beak, almost 3,000 army personnel were detailed to construct 170 fighter pens, 31 naval aircraft pens, 70 pens for reconnaissance aircraft and fourteen large bomber pens as well as twenty-seven miles of dispersal runways.

***Feldmarschall* Kesselring went ahead with plans for an all-out aerial assault to capture Malta.**

Detachments of the Royal West Kents and the Buffs were based at Luqa with the Manchesters at Ta'Qali and the Devonshire Regiment at Hal Far. Their brief was to build solid bombproof holding areas using rubble and masonry. Working twelve-hour shifts on half-rations and only taking cover during raids, the u-shaped shelters were initially sandbagged and then reinforced with discarded oil drums filled with earth before enough stone was eventually found to make the structures

RAF personnel work around the clock to construct aircraft shelters.

permanent. The best examples of these can be seen in fields alongside the new dual carriageway on the plain below Rabat that links Zeebug to Golden (formerly Military) Bay. They did their job sufficiently well enough that by the end of February 1942, the RAF was confident enough to consider allowing Spitfires to join the Battle of Malta.

Kesselring's all-out aerial assault of Malta still showed no signs of abating however and, spurred on by General Student, the planning of the invasion of Malta (Operation Hercules) continued, though Kesselring was becoming an increasingly moderate voice on the Axis side among those around him. Field Marshal Rommel had previously stated that the capture of Malta was essential if his march through North Africa was not to stall. But his stunning victory at Tobruk, where he captured intact huge supplies of petrol, provisions and ammunition as well as vehicles, appeared to inspire him to throw caution to the desert wind and he pressed Berlin for an immediate invasion of Egypt in a bid to capture the Suez Canal. His request by-passed the Italian High Command, technically his superiors,

Flushed with victories in North Africa, Rommel sought Hitler's permission to drive into Egypt and capture the Suez Canal.

but Mussolini seemed unconcerned. After all, he'd already ordered his dress uniform, white charger and ceremonial sword for a planned triumphal entrance through the gates of Cairo and not even Kesselring's reservations about overstretching the *Afrika Korps'* supply lines was going to spoil planning for his big day.

Egypt, meanwhile, was to be the initial destination of more than forty Maltese internees thought to have Italian sympathies, among them Chief Justice and President of the Maltese Court of Appeal, Arturo Mercieca, and Dr Mitzi, leader of the Malta Nationalist Party. Mercieca had refused to sever his Italian connections at the start of the war and been placed under house arrest at his family home in Naxxar after both he and Mizzi had publicly voiced pro-Italian and anti-British sentiments at a time when national unity was called for.

Dr Mitzi, leader of the Malta Nationalist Part

As the conflict became more intense, Mercieca and his associates had to be interned to prevent the possibility of information being passed to the enemy and the party was eventually deported to Uganda where they saw out the war in relative luxury before being repatriated in 1945.

Convoy MW-10

Early in 1940, at the height of the Battle of Britain, the Maltese people had given generously to an appeal for funds towards the construction of Spitfires. The fact that none of these sleek fighting machines had yet been sent to Malta had not gone down well with the islanders, who regarded themselves as British citizens entitled to the best defence their country could muster in their hour of need. So it was with great celebration that the Maltese greeted the rumours of the aircraft's imminent deployment in March 1942. Unfortunately, rumours were still all they were at this point in time.

Kesselring's invasion plans were well known to the British and, as the bombing became even more intense, fears were again raised that an airborne assault was about to be launched from Sicily by the Italians. Hitler still remained sceptical about his allies' capabilities, however, and would only agree to a nominal German supporting force while priorities lay elsewhere. So the invasion was again put on hold.

The *Luftwaffe* was now dropping an average of almost 7,000 tons of munitions a month on the airfields of Malta, and had even been using high explosives (known as JABO projectiles) to attack the cliffs beneath Mdina, facing Ta'Qali airfield, after receiving intelligence that reinforced bunkers had been dug into the limestone. These reports were of course false, but the RAF ground crew at Ta'Qali were hugely entertained to see the Stukas fly over their exposed positions to bomb an innocuous cliff face.

The Maltese authorities had now introduced a system of red warning flags during raids to let the people know it was safe to continue working outside target areas, but the islanders were still getting little relief from the convoys.

The armed tanker the *Breconshire* had made many runs to Malta from Alexandria with her precious cargo of fuel oil. But her luck finally ran out as part of Convoy MW-10 when she was so badly damaged she had to be towed into Marsaxlokk Bay, listing with her engine-room flooded and without power, steering and lights. Despite several attempts to stabilise her, Captain Hutchison and his exhausted crew had to be taken off and she was scuttled with depth charges the next day, along with her cargo.

The *Clan Campbell* was also sunk, with the loss of thirty-seven of her crew, twelve miles out of Grand Harbour but the *Pampas* and the Norwegian-registered *Talabot* made it to their berths under the Barrakka Gardens, despite the fact that their escorts had had to leave them to fend for themselves at the harbour entrance. The former had some amazing luck as described by crewman John Mulligan in David A. Thomas' *Malta Convoys:*

> *One enemy plane found us, unprotected, and dropped a stick of three bombs. The first one hit the derrick over the aviation spirit drums and just disintegrated, the second hit the starboard side of the funnel about ten feet from where we were standing, ricocheted across the boat deck and over the side and the third one missed the boat by a yard or two.*

The *Pampas* and the *Talabot* had also sailed right through the middle of a minefield without mishap in their haste to find refuge but their crews' efforts were almost all in vain. The decision was taken to only unload the ships while there was light and leave the work to the Maltese stevedores. But both ships came under heavy attack the following day, with a fierce fire taking hold on board the *Talabot*. As she was carrying a cargo containing ammunition, the *Talabot* had to be scuttled to lessen the risk of an explosion, though more than 1,000 tons of her load, including valuable flour, was later salvaged after she'd settled on the bottom of Grand Harbour. The ship's bell was also rescued and is now an exhibit at the National War Museum.

Wing Commander Powell-Sheldon, station commander at

Leutnant Johannes Geiseman alongside the rudder of his Ju88 which indicates ten ships sunk, amounting to almost 80,000 tons in one year, August 1941 to August 1942.

Luqa, had himself meanwhile taken matters in hand concerning the *Pampas*. She was carrying spares needed to patch up operational aircraft so Powell-Sheldon ordered a party of RAF ground crew and naval personnel as well as 100 men from the Cheshires, who were guarding Luqa, to go to the docks and help the locals. In the end, the combined effort managed to get almost 4,000 tons of cargo onto dry land before the Pampas, too, went to the bottom.

April 1942 was turning out to be the darkest month in Malta's modern history.

Though HMS *Penelope*, severely damaged in escorting Convoy MW-10, again proved an example of how proficient the Maltese dockyards were when she was deemed fit enough to sail for Egypt on 8 April 1942, a day earlier the Maltese had lost one of their most famous and revered landmarks.

HMS *Penelope.*

Malta, George Cross

Valletta's Opera House, standing in what is now Republic Square but was then the top of Kingsway (formerly the Strada Reale), dated from 1862 and was the focal point for not only grand theatre in Malta but also Valletta's traditional Carnival Day.

Designed by Edward Middleton Barry, architect of London's Covent Garden, the Opera House was eventually opened in 1866 only to be partly destroyed by fire in 1873.

The exterior of the Opera House escaped relatively unscathed and, after four years, performances were again taking place in front of more than 1,000 patrons on a regular basis, the theatre gaining a reputation throughout Europe for its flawless productions. But its grand pillars, intricately decorated colonnade and ornate carvings were no defence against the bombs of the Luftwaffe and, on the evening of Tuesday 7 April the imposing edifice took several hits.

To the residents of Valletta, this latest blow was hard to take. The roof of the national theatre was left a mesh of twisted metal. Girders had crashed into the auditorium and the elegant portico lay in ruins. There was no shortage of volunteers willing to help save what was left of this magnificent building but damage to the bridge crossing the Great Ditch at the nearby Porta Reale (City Gate) had restricted access to the area and this was also of great concern to the authorities as it provided the main thoroughfare out of Valletta into Floriana.

Valletta's Opera House House before and after 7 April 1942.

The structures were stabilised, however, and the site eventually cleared of rubble. Several offers to rebuild the Opera House were to be turned down in the post-war years (including one by German ex-PoWs) and subsequent Maltese governments have deferred a decision on whether or not it would be feasible to rebuild the theatre so it remains today, albeit unwittingly, a monument to the fortitude of the Maltese people under siege, though there are still signs that the Opera House hasn't yet finished fulfilling the role it was built for.

Yet for all that the destruction of the Opera House had demoralised the Maltese, they were lifted again by a miraculous escape for the congregation inside Mosta's Church of St Mary just two days later. Mosta's magnificent domed roof, the third largest unsupported dome in world, dates from the 1860s and is arguably one of the most beautiful churches in the Mediterranean. How it survived to this day has

Bomb damage outside Valletta's City Gate.

Mosta's famed dome.

become known as 'The Miracle of Mosta'. There were more than 300 people attending early evening mass when the sirens sounded on 9 April 1942. Most of these devout Catholics decided that not even the *Luftwaffe* was going to interrupt their prayers and the majority opted to stay inside the church rather than race for the shelters, after all Mosta wasn't usually a target for the bombers despite its proximity to Grand Harbour and Ta'Qali. This was not an ordinary day, however, and the congregation was shocked to hear the whistle of falling bombs get nearer and nearer, seconds before two tremendous clangs echoed around the gold-plated rotunda. Two 200kg bombs had hit the roof and been deflected into the Pjazza Rotunda below – neither exploded. Seconds later, a third bomb, released by a second aircraft, pierced the domed ceiling and thudded into the wall adjacent to the altar where the priest was knelt in prayer.

There was total silence as it skittled down the aisle between the pews before rolling to a stop in the sacristy. It, too, had failed to detonate and, having been carried a safe distance from the church by brave members of

The Church of St Publius in 1943
and, inset, as it looks today.

the congregation, was eventually defused by a bomb disposal team. No-one received so much as a scratch and a replica of that bomb can still seen inside the Church of St Mary to this day as a reminder of how the people of Mosta were 'saved' – maybe God was on Malta's side after all.

The Maltese still needed convincing that Britain was taking the island's plight seriously though and, in that respect, King George VI's decision (prompted by Lord Mountbatten) to award the George Cross to Malta, the first and only time a whole nation had been awarded this highest civilian bravery medal, was well timed, though it was to be September before the honour could be officially accepted on behalf of the islanders by the Chief Justice of Malta, Sir George Borg. In a ceremony in Palace Square, Valletta, more than 4,000 Maltese gathered to cheer proceedings before the medal and accompanying inscription was sent on a tour of the island's cities and villages. It is now on permanent display at the National War Museum alongside the French Curtain wall beneath St Elmo.

To Honour her brave people I award the George Cross to the Island Fortress of Malta: to bear witness to a heroism and devotion that will long be famous in History.

King George VI, 15th April 1942.

Sir George Borg accepts the George Cross on behalf of Malta and its people.

At last, some serious muscle for the defence of Malta, 48 Spitfires are loaded onto the American aircraft carrier the USS *Wasp* for transporting to the Meditterranean.

Spitfires

On the Clyde three days prior to the 'Miracle of Mosta', forty-eight Spitfires had been loaded onto the giant carrier *USS Wasp* along with pilots from 601 and 603 Squadrons. On the morning of 20 April, forty-seven of those aircraft arrived safely at Ta'Qali and Luqa following a four-hour flight.

They joined the vanguard of fifteen embattled Spitfires that had been flown in off HMS *Eagle* six weeks earlier, and been in constant action since, but their arrival hadn't gone unnoticed and their young pilots, drawn from nations as far apart as New Zealand and the USA, had barely had time to sit down to lunch in the Officers' Mess that doubled as an operations

USS *Wasp*.

control room at the Pointe De Vue Guest House on the main road to Rabat and Mdina when a combination of strafing Me109s, Ju87s and Ju88s swooped from the clouds.

The RAF ground crew managed to get six Spitfires, which had already been refuelled, and the same number of Hurricanes airborne before they had to run for the shelters. But the defenders couldn't prevent the total destruction of twenty of the newly arrived Spitfires with twelve more

Spitfires prepare to fly to Malta's aid.

Pointe De Vue Guest House (right) acted as control room and mess at Ta'Qali. It still stands today.

suffering substantial damage. Wing Commander Jack Satchell DFC, Station Commander at Ta'Qali, could only watch in frustration from the cliffs above as the new Spitfires burned on the plain below. It was to be a harsh lesson in reality for his rookie pilots.

The Supermarine Spitfire remains Britain's most endearing symbol of aerial defiance. The only Allied fighter to remain in production throughout the entirety of World War II, R. J. Mitchell's streamlined brainchild, developed by his Chief Draughtsman Joe Smith, had elliptical wings that gave it a speed advantage over the Hurricane and also allowed the aircraft to perform steep turns at the point of stall, meaning it could usually outmanoeuvre its main adversary, the Me109, at close quarters though, until the invention of a metal diaphragm known as Mrs Shilling's Orifice (named after engineer Beatrice Shilling) which solved the problem of fuel starvation to its Merlin engine, it was vulnerable when forced to dive.

There were twenty-four variations of the Spitfire in its service life with five different wing designs which utilised a variety of weapons. Generally, however, they were equipped with a combination of .303 machine guns and 20mm cannon, though later variations carried two .50-inch Browning heavy machine guns. The Mark V was the most common type and it was those that had flown off HMS *Eagle* and the USS *Wasp* in spring 1942, though technicians on the island hadn't been enamoured to discover they would have to reconfigure the guns, which had been hastily assembled out of sync with the aircraft's propeller.

However, the Spitfire's ever-increasing presence on Malta came too late to save Sir William Dobbie's position as Governor. Dobbie had taken the plight of the Maltese people to heart, even though he too had shared their hardships. Dobbie's health, physically and mentally, had begun to fail and, despite a vote of confidence from his paymasters in Cairo in March, a visit by Acting Minister of State Lord Monckton and Air Marshal Tedder, the AOC Middle East, (prompted by the influential editor of the *Times of Malta*, Mabel Strickland) in April confirmed the reports emanating out of Malta that Dobbie was no longer capable of co-ordinating its defence. Lieutenant Governor Sir Edward Jackson was already making the majority of the administrative decisions without consulting his immediate superior, but it was thought that he lacked the diplomatic experience to be made Governor and the job was given to Lord John Gort.

Gort had won the Military Cross and a VC in the First World War and had more of a military background than his predecessor, but he'd been in something of a political wilderness (as Governor of Gibraltar) since, as Commander-in-Chief, he'd overseen the retreat of the ill-fated British Expeditionary Force from Dunkerque. He was later to be accused of lacking compassion for the Maltese people and of being obsessed with military strategy though, to be fair, he arrived on the island amidst a worsening crisis in terms of rations and the disintegration of the islands' infrastructures.

Lord John Gort VC.

Malta's capital city suffered massive damage.

More than 700 people had lost their lives since the turn of the year, with another 1,000 injured. Floriana, adjoining Valletta, was now taking heavy punishment with the Church of St Publius sustaining damage along with the commercial district, lining what is now known as the Triq Sant Anna, the main thoroughfare out of Valletta towards the Porte des Bombes. There was a tragedy at St Paul's Old People's Home in Hamrun, where thirty-eight patients

The Id-Duka ta York still shows the scars of war, but new build is now springing up from the old.

and staff died when one of the wings received a direct hit, and at Zetjun, where twenty-one died when the town square was bombed.

More than half of the houses in the densely populated areas of Malta had suffered total destruction with the Three Cities, adjacent to the dockyards, worse affected. Observers likened the waterfronts to something that had been only previously seen at places like Ypres on the Western Front during the First World War and even today some buildings are still little more than shells despite extensive recent redevelopment. Walking past the Lascaris War Rooms on the road towards Floriana out of Valletta and down Id-Duka ta York behind the cafes and bars of the port's new cruise terminal, one can still see excellent examples of this.

The docks themselves could now only offer superficial help to shipping. Fabrication work still went on, but welders could only work in underground shelters so the sparks from their equipment didn't act as a pathfinder to the Luftwaffe, who could almost come and go as they pleased considering they outnumbered the RAF ten to one.

Even worse, the implications were obvious when reconnaissance over Sicily had uncovered the building of two glider strips. Student was again pressing Hitler to sanction Operation Hercules, with reconnaissance flights increased and plans made to combine the German's *7th Air Division* with the *Italian Folgore Division*. That would have been a total of 30,000 airborne troops, the same number of servicemen that Britain had its disposal in the entire Maltese islands.

More than 500 Ju52s were to provide the transport needs of the invasion force, but again, with the Germans seemingly poised to take Malta out of the equation once and for all, Hitler vetoed the plan ordering his offensive aircraft to support operations in Russia and North Africa instead. Suddenly, it was Italian SM79s overflying the island instead of Ju87s and the number of raids was dramatically reduced. Germany's last chance to put a stranglehold on Britain's Mediterranean operations had gone and, though no one knew this at the time, the cartoonists back in Britain were having a field day.

The lack of supplies was still threatening to end Malta's resistance, however, only the ill-fated Convoy MW-10 had got through to Malta since the turn of the year and, despite the efforts of submarines and the minelayer HMS *Welshman*, they were limited by storage space in what they could bring in. It wouldn't be inaccurate to say that the collective cupboard was now virtually bare.

More air cover was needed so that any convoys that did risk running

German map of Malta memorialising a bomber crew.

A Spitfire in its blast shelter.

the Mediterranean gauntlet could be unloaded. May 9th brought that air cover and the RAF showed they had learned their lesson of the previous month, when newly arrived aircraft were attacked as they landed. Again the USS *Wasp* and HMS *Eagle* were the platforms from which sixty-four Spitfires took off. All but two reached their destination, but this time they were greeted on the runway by motorcyclists and cyclists with numbers on their backs. The Spitfires were led immediately to the recently strengthened blast pens where mechanics would give them a brief inspection before they were rearmed and refuelled. The new aircraft were then sent on patrol, piloted by a Malta veteran. Within half-an-hour of landing, sixty-one of the sixty-two Spitfires were back in the air and successfully repelling a succession of raids.

Nine days later, further RAF reinforcements arrived on the island – Germany and Italy no longer had air supremacy, the tide had finally turned in the skies over Malta.

Cartoonists in London revel in the Axis failure to subdue Malta.

Chapter Nine

THE SANTA MARIJA CONVOY

We are determined that Malta shall not be allowed to fall. The starving out of this fortress would involve the surrender of over 30,000 men. Its possession would give the enemy a clear and sure bridge to Africa, with all the consequences flowing from that.

Winston Churchill, May 7th, 1942

WITH sporadic power cuts, some lasting several days, and bread rationing reduced even further (the average man in the street was now down to what equated to a slice and a half a day), there was little to cheer the Maltese in the summer of 1942. The Germans and Italians were no longer mounting raids around the clock, but they were still pounding Grand Harbour and the airfields on a regular basis and any attempt to lift the siege was met with massive force.

Air Vice-Marshal Lloyd was adopting a hands-on approach with his new pilots, leaving the comparative safety of RAF HQ in Balluta Bay (now St Julians) to visit Ta'Qali, Luqa or Hal Far in the middle of a raid and refusing to take cover while bombs dropped around his staff car. There were no barracks intact to house the new 603 Squadron and many airmen had to sleep in tents in olive groves, which still stand today opposite the vineyards next to Ta'Qali. Even so the pilots' morale remained high. In James Douglas-Hamilton's book *The Air Battle for Malta,* David (Later Lord) Douglas-Hamilton described his feelings in a letter home;

You will have gathered from the Press and News that we have raids every day and pretty heavy ones at that, but this place still holds out and will continue to hold out.

But they wouldn't hold out for much longer without supplies and the relative failure of Operations Harpoon and Vigorous, launched simultaneously from opposite ends of the Mediterranean in June, merely compounded Malta's plight.

Of those vessels that departed Gibraltar, only two freighters, the SS *Troilus* and the SS *Orari*, survived a prolonged action with the *Regia Navale* and subsequent bombing raids by the *Luftwaffe*, despite the presence of carriers HMS *Eagle* and HMS *Argus*, while the Alexandria convoy turned back after being attacked repeatedly by Ju87s and Ju88s and harassed by Italian E-boats.

The Governor's Palace had a lucky escape when a parachute bomb

St John's Co-Cathedral as a backdrop to bomb damage around Palace Square and (above), St John's today.

exploded on the opposite side of Kingsway, causing widespread destruction across Palace Square, the concussion bringing down a wall of St John's Co-Cathedral a little further up Kingsway. Thankfully, the magnificent cathedral was able to be fully restored but the popular Capitol cinema didn't enjoy the same fortune. Shops next door took a direct hit and the picture house was so badly damaged it had to be pulled down.

More than 1,200 Maltese civilians had now died in raids, with a further 3,000 injured. More bombs had fallen on the island in three years than fell on London during the entire Second World War. To try and deflect attacks away from the few ships still using Grand Harbour, the Royal Malta Artillery had begun experimenting with smoke canisters to confuse enemy aircraft, though the larger number of fighters based in Malta had also begun to make an impact on the effectiveness of the raiders. But it was the lack of air cover outside of the normal range of the Hurricanes and Spitfires that was the problem area for the British. They couldn't protect shipping at the Western end of the Mediterranean from German and Italian aircraft based in Sardinia and Sicily.

Areas bordering the dockyards were worst hit.

Queen Victoria's statue looks across a devastated Palace Square.

Military casualties on Malta were still rising and the Royal Navy made the unprecedented step of getting a message to the Italians, requesting permission for a hospital ship to evacuate the more seriously injured from Valletta. The *Regia Navale* agreed, but Mussolini would have nothing of it and, backed up by the Germans, refused. The wounded would have to continue their treatment at Mtarfa and the Royal Naval Hospital at Bighi in Kalkara. In common with Barrakka, Bighi once had a tower lift in operation

Bighi Hospital with its lift in the foreground.

to transport casualties and supplies from sea level to the hospital grounds. Surprisingly, both structures survived the war largely intact though only the towers themselves now remain.

On 20 June 1942, Rommel's Afrika Korps finally overran Tobruk and another safe haven for Allied shipping in the Mediterranean had gone. Gort and the authorities had to prepare for the worst.

It was estimated that, even with reduced rations, Malta's populations only had enough food to last until the end of August 1942 and that was set as the target date by which the island would be forced to surrender if relief was not forthcoming. All householders were ordered to declare stocks of essential goods they'd managed to store but the situation wasn't being helped by an increase in petty pilfering (largely sparked by desperation rather than profit) of supplies, particularly fuel, and a gibbet was even constructed outside Ta'Qali accompanied by notices warning that theft from government installations was punishable by death under military law. The War Office were furious when photographs of the gibbet appeared in the British press, as it was felt that it gave a false impression of the treatment the armed forces handed out to people it was supposed to be defending from tyranny. Mercifully, however, the scaffold was never used.

Operation Pedestal was Malta's last throw of the dice. A.V. Alexander, the First Lord of the Admiralty, left the captains of the convoy in no doubt of that as he addressed them in Gibraltar on the evening of 10 August.

> *Before you start on this operation, the First Sea Lord and I are anxious that you should know how grateful the Board of Admiralty is to you for undertaking this difficult task. Malta has for some time been in great danger. It is imperative she should be kept supplied. These are her critical months, and we cannot fail her. She has stood up to the most violent attack from the air that has ever been made and now she needs our help in continuing the battle. Her courage is worthy of yours.*

Assembled for the convoy's protection was the most powerful fleet ever seen for an operation of this nature. Sixty-four warships, including the aircraft carriers *Victorious*, *Eagle*, *Indomitable* and *Furious*, battleships *Nelson* and *Rodney*, cruisers *Phoebe*, *Sirius*, *Charybdis*, *Nigeria*, *Kenya*, *Manchester* and *Cairo*; thirty-three destroyers and half-a-dozen submarines were detailed to protect fourteen of the largest-yet-most-manoeuvrable freighters in service with, or on secondment to, the Merchant Navy. They included the US-registered tanker *Ohio*, which was carrying more than 11,000 tons of kerosene and oil.

The convoy slipped out of Gibraltar in thick fog on Thursday 11 August but disaster struck almost immediately. Such a large formation couldn't hope to avoid detection for long and the Axis forces were given plenty of advance warning of the convoy's move into the Mediterranean. As a result, almost 400 Ju87s and Ju88s were poised to wreak havoc on the British forces, supported by squadrons of SM79s and E-boats. In addition U-boats, based in the south of France, had increased their patrols and it was one of

HMS *Victorious* leading HMS *Eagle* viewed from HMS *Indomitable* in the early stages of Operation Pedestal before the Axis onslaught.

those, U-73, that was to strike the first blow against Operation Pedestal.

Amidst an attack by forty Stukas, the U-73 fired a four-torpedo spread and scored a direct hit on the *Eagle* with devastating results. Petty Officer Ellis, on board the *Nigeria*, described what happened in David A Thomas' *Malta Convoys*:

> *During a lull in the action I was watching the Eagle's planes take off. Then a muffled boom and she just slipped over. The planes on her deck began to slide into the water. I got a bit busy and the next time I glanced astern all I could see were a couple of destroyers picking up survivors."*

With the *Furious*, who was originally only intended as a forward launch platform for more fighters for Malta, also sustaining damage and turning back after fulfilling her role, the convoy's carrier escort was halved straight away. The *Eagle* had gone down in minutes with all but four of her aircraft still on board, along with 260 of her crew.

The following day brought even more sustained attacks; a wave of Ju88s arrived at dawn, swiftly followed by a larger contingent of German and Italian bombers armed with torpedoes. One of these sank the SS *Deucalion*.

Another wave of thirty Ju87s dived out of the clouds and the *Indomitable* was struck three times. The destroyer *Foresight* was so badly holed that she had to be abandoned and sunk. The cruisers *Cairo* and *Nigeria* were torpedoed by Italian submarines and also suffered severe damage, the former abandoned and the latter forced to turn back to Gibraltar. Just as significantly, the tanker *Ohio* had been hit and was reported on fire. But her crew knew that she had to make Malta at all costs and the fire was eventually brought under control, though the damage incurred meant she could only make 13 knots.

As darkness fell, the Ju88s returned and the SS *Empire Hope* joined the casualty list, her cargo of high-octane gas being ignited by a bomb. A huge explosion also destroyed the SS *Clan Ferguson*, which had been carrying a

Men can be seen crowding the starboard side of HMS *Eagle* seconds before the ship heels over and sinks.

Ju88s – they proved to be effective in the anti-shipping role.

large stock of ammunition, while the SS *Brisbane Star*, which had already been bombed, and the cruiser *Kenya* were also struck by torpedoes. The *Brisbane Star's* bows were almost torn from her hull but, miraculously, there was no fire and she managed to stay afloat. A bomb then struck the carrier *Indomitable*, the blast causing mayhem among her forward AA gun turrets, killing seventy-two of her crew, many of them Royal Marines.

The morning light of 13 August saw the convoy pass through the narrows off Sicily where Italian E-boats were in wait. The cruiser *Manchester* was so badly damaged that she had sunk by nightfall, but she lasted longer than the SS *Glenorchy* and SS *Wairangi*, who went down

Another escort carrier, HMS *Indomitable, is* targeted by enemy bombers.

quickly after being torpedoed. Though the crew of the latter were fortunate in that the destroyer *Eskimo* was almost alongside when she was struck and able to save all hands.

The American cargo ships *Santa Elisa* and *Almeria Lykes* were next to be targeted, the former catching fire and causing the crew to abandon. The latter was struck amidships by a torpedo and sank almost immediately.

The *Rochester Castle* was also torpedoed, but was able to carry out running repairs and got under way again. By now the convoy was in range of Malta-based fighters, but they were unable to communicate with the escorts and were themselves fired upon as they flew in from the east in an attempt to engage a dozen Ju88s who were pressing home yet another attack. The Ju88s found their target; a cluster and bombs, which killed nearly all of her officers, struck the *Waimarrama's* bridge. Secondary explosions detonated her cargo of aviation fuel and ammunition and she went under still ablaze with eighty-seven of her crew. The destroyer HMS *Leadbury* managed to rescue a lucky few who survived the inferno. Burning debris also set alight the *Melbourne Star* but she managed to emerge from the surface oil burning fiercely around her and keep her engines going.

Focus now switched to the *Ohio*. The Germans knew the value of her cargo and had no intention letting her reach her destination. Some sixty Stukas, described like bees around a honey-pot, tore into the remaining ships, many of them aiming at the American tanker *The Ohio*, almost 500 feet long and displacing 9,263 tons, it was one of the largest vessels of her

The *Ohio* before the attack.

The *Ohio* begins to take damage.

type and capable of transporting 170,000 barrels of oil at a steady 16 knots. But she wasn't designed to withstand the punishment the *Luftwaffe* were intent on handing out. Several near misses buckled her bow plates and the forward tank began to take in water. A stricken Ju88, disabled by the *Ohio's* own guns, crashed into her superstructure, swiftly followed by a burning Ju87, which attempted to crash-land on the water but only succeeded in crumpling against the tanker's hull. More bombs rained around her, two exploding simultaneously on either side of the big tanker and almost lifting her bodily out of the water. Her boilers gave up the fight and her back was all but broken but the crew and her escort still refused to give up the unequal struggle.

Meanwhile, the SS *Dorset* had become the latest casualty – she was abandoned after her engine-room flooded and a fire broke out among her cargo of gas. The cruiser *Kenya* too had caught fire, but that was quickly extinguished and she was able to make headway under own steam within two hours.

Back on the *Ohio*, desperate attempts were being made to attach a line for towing but she was rocked again when a U-boat torpedo found its mark in her centre section.

Chief Officer Gray of the Ohio reported:

When the torpedo struck the ship she shook violently. The steering gear broke and all communication with the engine room and the after end of the ship was cut off with the exception of a telephone.

Malta Convoys, David A Thomas.

Still the Ju88s attacked, determined to send the *Ohio* to the bottom. A bomb exploded in almost exactly the same spot as the torpedo, ripping a huge hole out of her main deck. The ship's bulkheads groaned in protest as the oil tank lids buckled and lay her precious cargo open to the elements, and the bombs. Fires were raging on board and the crew were forced to abandon ship as SM79s of the *Regia Aeronautica* carried on the assault. But the Italians were beaten off by a combination of AA fire and fighter support from Malta, which was now tantalisingly just over the horizon.

The *Ohio* was still afloat, so Captain Mason and his men returned to damp down the fires while her engineers assessed the damage below decks. Somehow, the Ohio still survived, and the Royal Navy wasn't about to desert the tanker and her crew. Destroyers HMS *Penn* and HMS *Ledbury* had already been detailed to give whatever aid they could, HMS *Rye* and HMS *Bramham* joined them.

By mid-morning 14 August, the *Penn* and the *Bramham* had been lashed to the Ohio to act as makeshift floats. A tow had been attached to the *Rye*, while the *Ledbury*

The ships *Penn* and the *Bramham* were lashed to the *Ohio* to keep her afloat.

Captain Mason skipper of the *Ohio*.

The *Ohio* and her escorts limp into Grand Harbour.

was nudging the *Ohio's* stern. A bomb blast had destroyed the tanker's rudder and she needed to be pointed in the right direction. With minesweepers *Hebe*, *Hythe* and *Speedy* fanned out in the vanguard, the flotilla inched toward Malta despite her sinking lower and lower in the water with the passing of each agonising hour.

Massive crowds, meanwhile, had lined the streets and walls around Grand Harbour as news began to spread about the convoy's imminent arrival and more were arriving by the minute with cries of 'Wasal il-konvoy!' (The convoy is here!). Spontaneous applause broke out among those perched on Abercrombie's Bastion as the *Port Chalmers*, flags flying, steamed into view on the morning of the 13th – she had survived relatively unscathed. The cheers got louder with the arrival of the *Rochester Castle*, though the crowds were hushed momentarily as they saw the size of the hole in her side. That afternoon, the *Melbourne Star*, her hull scarred by fire and pockmarked by shrapnel, reached port to be met by a frenzy of excitement.

Wing Commander Sandy Johnstone, who was working as a Flight Controller at the time, describes the scene in James Douglas-Hamilton's *The Air Battle for Malta*:

> *The Maltese went mad in a frenzied outburst of tears, laughter and loud unrestrained cheering. Young boys and girls leapt and screamed, while their parents roared themselves hoarse as they watched the long-awaited convoy gliding into safety. Old and young hugged and kissed each other, a few people just stood quietly, the tears of relief rolling unashamedly down their cheeks.*

The siege is lifted.

The crowds were reluctant to leave, even after nightfall, as though they didn't wish to desert the ships and their crews attempting to deliver the islands' salvation.

But they were back at first light the following day in hope of welcoming more of the convoy into harbour. In the Upper and Lower Barrakka Gardens, along the Triq Santa Barbara and on the opposite shore, beneath Fort St Angelo and around Dockyard Creek, huge numbers lined the shoreline. Children burrowed their way to the front to get a better view, chattering excitedly. The mood was sombre on the whole, however, with everyone peering out across the shimmering sea, while prayers were being said, in private as well as in churches, across the capital. Just after 3.00pm, their patience was rewarded as the *Brisbane Star* limped past the breakwater. Able Seaman Bob Sanders, again in David A Thomas' *Malta Convoys*, describes the final hours before his ship reached safety:

> *They threw everything at us. The planes came in droves of a hundred, and submarines tried to get us too. You did your watch then went straight to getting ammunition for the gunners from the lockers. People ask if you were scared. You went past that stage. You went on automatic.*

With a gaping hole in her bow, the *Brisbane Star's* arrival brought the crowds to a new level of excitement. People crammed into launches and djhajsas to greet her. The freighter's master, Captain Frederick Neville-Riley DSO, had performed heroics to save his ship and her crew. After being struck by the torpedo, he'd steered a course close to the Tunisian coast to mask the *Brisbane's Star* outline against the dark mountains. Now that the ordeal was over and he saw what Operation Pedestal meant to the Maltese, his composure cracked and a few tears were shed on the bridge that afternoon.

Again, the crowds were reluctant to leave that night, prepared to risk being caught in the open by a raid. But the people of Valletta and the Three Cities had to wait until the following day for the drama to be fully played out.

The *Ohio* and her escorts finally reached the entrance to Grand Harbour at nine o'clock on the morning of Saturday 15 August, the date of the Feast of the Assumption of Our Lady Mary, one of the most holy days in Malta's religious calendar. Her decks were awash and the wreckage of a Ju88 was still embedded in what remained of her twisted and charred superstructure, but she was still afloat, albeit almost broken in two, and much of her precious cargo was still intact.

Even as she passed the breakwater, the locals still didn't believe she was going to reach her berth alongside Parlatorio Wharf, however. The tug *Robust* and minesweepers *Beryl* and *Swona* had gone to her aid for, as she rounded Delimira Point, her towline had snapped. Drifting, the *Robust* tried to correct her drift, but collided with HMS *Penn* and it wasn't until the arrival of further seagoing tugs that the *Ohio* was finally moving in the right direction again and away from the minefields.

Unloading her valuable cargo, the Rochester Castle, a survivor of Operation Pedestal.

Charles B. Grech who, along with the band of the Royal Marines, was among the melee in the Lower Barrakka Gardens, repeats an argument he overheard in *Raiders Passed*:

> *One said that even if it made it up to the breakwater, it would not manage to get past the lanterns. Another gloomily predicted that, as soon as the destroyers cast off the lashing and towing cables, the tanker would go to the bottom. Yet another sea dog was of the opinion that it would be better if the tanker was not towed into harbour as there was probably nothing left inside its tanks, other than sea water.*

To the tune of 'Join the Navy and See the World', however, the *Ohio's* mooring lines were tied to capstans at 9.45am and she was safe. Captain Dudley Mason, who was awarded the George Cross for his efforts in getting the *Ohio* to Malta, and his crew had defied the odds and earned them the gratitude of a nation in the process. After having her tanks emptied, the *Ohio* was moored under Fort Rinella where she broke in two and settled in shallow water. She continued to be useful to the war effort, however, her stern being utilised as a diving base, while her forward section, having been made watertight, held naval stores for four years.

In September 1946, both halves were towed ten miles out to sea and the destroyer *Virago* ordered to sink her with its guns. The 'indestructible' *Ohio* wasn't going to go down without a fight however and, though her bow sank, her stern refused to follow and had to have depth-charges attached two weeks later to prevent her becoming a danger to shipping. The *Ohio* was finally at rest, but the Maltese will never forget the sacrifices made during 'The Santa Marija Convoy'.

Vice Admiral Neville Syfret wrote in dispatches;

> *The steadfast manner in which these ships pressed their way to Malta was a most inspiring sight. The memory of their conduct will remain an inspiration to all who were privileged to sail with them.*

Peter Smith, a leading authority on Malta's wartime role, described it as:

> *One of the small number of operations of the Second World War where you can say, without a doubt, that it alone made a difference.*

Artefacts, documents and photographs concerning 'The Santa Marija Convoy' and including the wheel of the *Ohio*, form part of a permanent exhibition at the National War Museum at the entrance to Fort St Elmo in Valletta.

Chapter Ten

ON THE ROAD TO SALVATION

MALTA AND ITS PEOPLE were by no means out of the woods, despite the vital supplies that Operation Pedestal had brought in, but there was finally a light at the end of the tunnel and the sight of the ships actually entering Grand Harbour had done wonders for national morale, among civilians and servicemen alike. There had been just 13 days left before Malta reached starvation point.

Optimism had now replaced pessimism and suddenly the gunners of the Royal Artillery and Royal Malta Artillery didn't have to count every shell. The Spitfires, including another seventy safely delivered by HMS *Furious,* and Hurricanes were able to fly round-the-clock patrols, and 227 Squadron's Beaufighters had arrived to increase the pressure on Rommel, as had Beauforts of 39 Squadron.

Beaufighter.

The Beaufighter, or Beau, was less manoeuvrable than the Spitfire but carried more in terms of firepower with its six .303 machine guns. It could also carry two 1000lb bombs or eight RP-3 rockets and was now able to operate day and night against targets in Sicily.

Beaufort.

Fortunes had taken a U-turn for the Afrika Corps' charismatic leader Rommel. With the lifting of the Malta siege, the British had resumed their attacks on the Germans' lines of logistic support with renewed vigour and the Malta-based submarine HMS *Umbra* was able to strike a mortal blow to Axis forces in North Africa when she sank the supply ship *Amsterdam,* which was crammed with tanks and trucks bound for Rommel.

It proved to be the beginning of the end for the Germans in North Africa. Within weeks, their advance had stalled at Alam Halfa and Montgomery's Eighth Army had turned near-certain defeat at El Alamein into a stunning victory. This potentially decisive setback was too much to take for Rommel, who was flown back to Austria suffering from stress and exhaustion. He was never to return and left behind an army in disarray.

Malta was now able to operate a blanket defence of aircraft and AA guns, giving the now returned Wellingtons and the submarine fleet based at Manoel Island much more freedom to launch attacks on supply lines. Bletchley Park's cracking of the Enigma codes meant that they could now pass on information to the communication centre at Lascaris about every ship leaving Italy for North Africa. The Afrika Corps was effectively cut off from the rest of the Third Reich. Vehicles were being abandoned in the desert where they'd run out of petrol and weapons, for which there was no ammunition, discarded.

Kesselring had one more card to play regarding Malta, however. Invasion was now out of the question, but he knew the Maltese were still desperately short of fuel and basic essentials, and believed that another blitz could still nullify the island as a base of offensive operations.

On the morning of 11 October, a large force of Ju88s, Macchi 202s and Me109s launched the first of several raids over the next few days. But they met an air defence that had been rejuvenated by Air Vice Marshal Sir Keith Park who, aided by a new and more advanced radar system at Dingli, had his aircraft engage the Luftwaffe over water rather than wait until the Germans began their bombing run. The envisaged final onslaught never really materialised, though Kesselring's final throw of the dice took a heavy toll on the Spitfires. More than fifty were shot down or put out of action inside three days, prompting new General Officer Commanding, Major General Scobie to draft an urgent request for new planes and pilots.

Scobie had thrown himself into his new job with vigour, but hadn't endeared himself to Lord Gort by suggesting that the Governor had concentrated too much on the needs of the military and ignored those of the civilian population. The Maltese winter, though rarely cold, invariably carries a dampening chill, and it was approaching fast. Many families were still homeless while others lived and slept in houses that had no fuel for heating or electricity for light, and most didn't even have glass in the windows.

Rations had improved slightly for the lifting of the siege in that there was more grain to bake bread and kerosene was more plentiful, but several prominent officials still expressed fears that civil unrest and even rioting were possible if the situation didn't begin to show marked improvement.

Most of the Victory Kitchens were still operating seven days a week and feeding more than 80,000 people and the authorities' decision to put liver, which the Maltese detested almost to a man, on the menu didn't aid matters – it was swiftly replaced by corned beef when the Communal Feeding Department was stormed.

Operation Stoneage alleviated the situation somewhat when arriving from Alexandria on 15 November. Despite being bombed (causing severe damage and loss of life on board the escorting cruiser HMS *Arethusa*), the merchant ships *Denbighshire*, *Bantam*, *Mormacmoon* and *Robin Locksley* safely delivered 35,000 tons of supplies and, though much of it was ammunition and aviation fuel, there was enough food to keep the population from going hungry. This was added to by another successful solo run from the ever-reliable HMS *Welshman*.

Despite being painted otherwise, Lord Gort wasn't unsympathetic to the Maltese plight and had been pressing the War Cabinet in Westminster for a grant to start rebuilding Malta. Operation Portcullis and Operation Quadrangle brought in another 175,000 tons of supplies before the turn of the year, easing the pressure on the Governor, and allowing luxuries like pork, mince pies and plum puddings to appear on the shelves before Christmas. The convoys also brought in barrage balloons for Grand Harbour; though this was probably a case of bolting the door after the horse had bolted, given that the air raids were becoming less and less frequent, the *Fliegerkorps X* having been removed to the Russian Front for the final time.

What the war had taught people on Malta, however, was that they could no longer rely totally on other nations to make decisions and fight battles on their behalf. The seeds of a new republic had been born in the railway tunnels of Floriana and the catacombs of Rabat, but politics would have to wait until peacetime.

JOURNEY INTO LIGHT – The Yanks are Coming

Operation Torch, the Allied landings in North Africa, had seen the United States officially enter the Western theatre for the first time and, with their arrival, Malta's safety was finally assured.

There were still shortages of course, and sporadic bombing raids, but

Allied forces make an amphibious landing near Algiers on 8 November, 1942. Few American troops based in Europe had been under fire, and they did not know whether Vichy French defenders would resist the landings.

the Italian bombers now arrived in groupings of no more than four or five, flying erratically to evade the fighters and dropped their loads hurriedly and without any real sense of purpose before high-tailing it back home. The boot was now definitely on the other foot by the beginning of 1943, with the emphasis switching from defence to attack as far as Malta's forces were concerned and Park's tactic of engaging the raiders over water had been of further benefit to civilians. Watching dogfights from the rooftops had become a massive spectator sport, particularly among the young, who would cheer every British success and groan when things were going badly. But it was common when gunfire was exchanged overhead for spent cartridges, stray shells and even debris to wound or even kill onlookers. With the 'action' taking place out at sea, that risk was largely negated, though the air-sea rescue launch based at St Paul's Bay, became increasingly important in rescuing downed pilots.

Badly damaged air-sea rescue launch in St Paul's Bay duing the siege.

The Victory Kitchens fed numbers in excess of 175,000 over Christmas 1942 but, with rations on the increase, those numbers had dwindled rapidly a month later. The Eighth Army was proving unstoppable in the deserts of North Africa, the drums and pipes of the Highlanders leading the march into Tripoli on 23 January, and German and Italian forces were starting to surrender in ever larger numbers. Some were placed at a temporary PoW camp at St Andrew's, adjacent to the army officers' mess and the British administration HQ at Pembroke.

St Paul's Bay.

Pembroke remained a

British base until 1979 but fell into a terrible state of repair when it was finally discarded and has only recently undergone extensive refurbishment. An international college now sits at its centre and, ironically, it's now one of the most sought after places to live alongside the area around Marsascala.

The Italians had all but given up trying to raise further convoys to supply their troops, concentrating now on the defence of their own sovereign territory. But even that task was beginning to look beyond the outmoded and out-gunned Regia Navale and Regia Aeronautica.

Three flights of converted Spitfires, loaded with 500lb bombs, had already inflicted severe damage on a chemical factory at Pachino in Sicily having flown from Hal Far and planning was already well advanced for Operation Husky, the invasion of Sicily itself by the Allies

There was sad news for the people of Malta at the beginning of February, however, when HMS *Welshman,* the fast minelayer that had run the gauntlet of Axis bombers so many times to bring relief to the islanders, was sunk off Tobruk with the loss of almost half of her crew. But the month did finally see the end of the bombing of Malta, though there was much too much to do for anyone to celebrate for long.

February 26 was the day the final 'Raiders Passed' signal was raised but it went virtually unnoticed as preparations were in full swing for the invasion of Sicily. Large invasion barges arrived in Marsamxett Harbour

Malta could be used as a base for Operation Husky, the invasion of Sicily. American troops with a specially designed beach landing craft and DKUW vehicle.

The Cheshire Regiment had seen action around the globe since being formed under the leadership of Henry, Duke of Norfolk on the Roodee alongside the River Dee in Chester in 1689.
Initially raised to oppose James II's ambitions to retake the English throne, the new force first saw action in Ireland where it was eventually garrisoned after fighting under the name of the 22nd Regiment of Foot in the Battles of Boyne and Aughrim. During the 1700s, the regiment sailed to Jamaica to battle both the French and local chieftains before seeing action in the Battle of Dettingen in the War of the Austrian Succession. Honours were subsequently earned on Martinique and in Cuba, and in the Battle of Bunker Hill, fighting to maintain British interests in New York and New Jersey.
Now renamed the Cheshire Regiment, a posting to South Africa in 1800 was followed by a prolonged active service in India, being stationed on Mauritius until after the demise of Napoleon Bonaparte. Engagements in Burma followed at the end of the 19th century before the regiment saw concerted action during the Boer War.
On August 24th 1914, the 1st Battalion suffered heavy casualties at Aurdegnies in the latter stages of the Battle of Mons but continued to fight on the Western Front for the entirety of WW1 with other detachments serving at Gallipoli and in Palestine.

and the loading of tanks and support vehicles began at the end of May. Major roads had been cleared of rubble around Grand Harbour, allowing a constant stream of traffic day and night while troops marched along The Strand in Sliema and from St Andrew's and St George's Barracks to their point of disembarkation.

It was noted that most of the invasion force looked fit and well nourished, unlike Malta's civilian population and garrison who were still trying to regain weight lost during the siege.

The men of the Kings Own Malta Regiment, many of them part-time soldiers, had suffered as much as the civilians, while battalions from the Royal Irish Fusiliers, the Buffs (the Royal East Kent's) and the Cheshires had spent long attachments on Malta and were undoubtedly battle-weary. After finally being relieved from their posting on Malta, the 1st Battalion the Cheshire Regiment were to go on and play a major part in the Allies' eventual victory forming part of the force that retook Benghazi and partaking in the defence of Egypt as well as the invasion of Sicily. In the aftermath of the D-Day landings, the Cheshires also helped establish bridgeheads in Normandy – a carved plaque in Vittoriosa commemorates their time on Malta.

After a short rest, they were to suffer heavy losses in fierce fighting on the island of Leros near Turkey, where Commanding Officer Lieutenant Colonel Maurice French was among the many who lost their lives.

Ironically, the 4th Battalion of the Buffs, who were stationed on Malta between 1940 and 1942, were also to suffer casualties in the ill-fated defence of Leros.

On the 26th May, for the first time in three years, a convoy sailed to Malta from Alexandria without losing a single ship. It

George VI visited in Valletta to view the damage for himself.

arrived alongside wharfs that were more rubble than structure, but now the stevedores were able to move freely along the quayside without fear of attack. Even at night, arc lights lit up Grand Harbour, allowing unloading of vital fuel, ammunition and foodstuffs to continue uninterrupted.

The following month brought another landmark as, amid tight security, King George VI arrived in Valletta to view the damage for himself. A plaque adjacent to the steps of Custom House on the Triq Pinto alongside Grand Harbour commemorates his visit, which took in a tour of the dockyards and a walk around the worst affected streets of Senglea.

British Prime Minister Winston Churchill

The Royal Irish Fusiliers, another stalwart in the defence of Malta, was first raised in response to the growing threat of the French at the end of the 18th century. Fighting Napoleon took the new regiment across Europe, North Africa, South America, the Caribbean and North America but their greatest triumph came at the Battle of Barossa in Spain, where Sergeant Masterman of the 87th Regiment returned from the field of engagement with the French Imperial Eagle.

Based in Armagh, by the end of the 19th century they found themselves in Egypt fighting the Mahdists at the Battle of Omdurman, before facing the Mahdi and his Arab forces in Sudan. The Boer War was to prove something of a disaster when, after the Battle of Tamana Hill, many of the men were either taken prisoner or trapped in the Siege of Ladysmith, large numbers dying of disease, while their commanders dithered.

The regiment fought at Gallipoli and in Palestine in WWI, and also saw action at Armentieres and Ypres, becoming one of the first British regiments to endure gas attacks. Joining forces with the Irish and Ulster Divisions, further casualties were suffered at the Battle of the Somme and at Cambrai. In the early days of WWII, the 1st Battalion were fighting their way to Dunkirk as part of the British Expeditionary Force, while the 2nd Battalion were stranded where they had been stationed in Malta, remaining on the island until they were relieved in June 1943.

Ship to shore taxiing boats.

commemorated with a bust in Palace Square, Valletta and USA President Franklin D. Roosevelt were to follow in the King's path by the end of 1943, but by then the Allies had invaded and conquered Sicily and were battling their way through mainland Italy.

Malta had become the launch pad for the invasion of Sicily, with landing craft tethered to every available mooring post and capstan. The Americans even building a new airfield on Gozo from which Spitfires were able to fly protection for the beachheads established on Italian soil.

Xewkija was completed inside two weeks, dual runways criss-crossing the site of two former farms south-east of the capital Victoria that had been purchased under the Emergency Act.

But the airfield was to have a short operational life. By early August, the Allies had 'liberated' and refurbished most of Sicily's airstrips, making Xewkija obsolete. The land was returned to the farmers from whom it was taken and nowadays one struggles to see any sign of its wartime role in the fields surrounding the ancient citadel.

Bust of wartime Prime Minister Winston Churchill.

September 1943 also brought a measure of revenge for the Maltese with

Malta became the base for the invasion of Sicily. Landing craft tethered to every available mooring post and capstan.

the surrender of the Italian fleet. With Mussolini overthrown and King Emmanuel signing an armistice with the Allies, the Germans were frantically trying to commandeer all of the Italian assets. But they couldn't reach the southern ports of Genoa, Spezia and Taranto before the Regia Navale fled and their nearest safe haven was Malta.

On the evening of Friday 10, the Italian battleship *Savoia*, under a flag of surrender, crept into St Paul's Bay in the gathering gloom flanked by two more battleships and destroyers. HMS *Warspite* was quickly on the scene and, on the morning of the 11th, arrangements were made with Admiral da

Custom House, St Paul's Bay, where the Italian fleet surrendered.

Zara, acting Commander-in-Chief of the Italian fleet at Taranto, for the formal surrender of his ships. At four o'clock precisely, a guard of honour from the *Warspite* greeted da Zara at the steps of Custom House in Valletta and he was whisked away. The car he was travelling in deliberately taking a circuitous route so that he became aware of the damage his fellow countrymen had inflicted on the island of Malta.

With the fall of Tunis and the invasion of Sicily, Malta's front-line role in World War II was all but over; there was just one more ceremony to perform. Almost a year after the raising of the second Great Siege of Malta, the skeleton of Gladiator N5520, which had been almost destroyed by a bomb at Hal Far, was discovered on wasteland at the Aircraft Repair Section at Kalafrana.

'Faith' had lost her wings but not the affection or gratitude of the Maltese people who lined up several deep around Palace Square in Valletta to see Sir Keith Park formally present the aircraft to Sir George Borg, who accepted her on behalf of Malta. It says much about 'Faith' and her fellow Gladiators of Station Flight that Italian reports, subsequently uncovered, believed Malta's aircraft defence at the start of the siege numbered more then twenty.

'Faith' is now housed permanently in the National War Museum, a fitting memorial to the bravery and resilience of a proud nation that doesn't know the meaning of surrender.

Gloster Gladiator *Faith*, minus wings, at the National War Museum, St Elmo fort.

Chapter Eleven

OPPOSING VIEWS

VICTORY for the Allies in Europe and the Far East brought peace for millions, but their British overlords quickly extinguished hopes that the Maltese Islands could be a part of the New World order. Had a confidential Colonial Office proposal from late 1942 been leaked, the Maltese would certainly have had an inkling that the British Government had no intention of allowing the winds of change to blow through the Mediterranean after the war. Lord Gort had already expressed the opinion that the world-wide admiration of the Maltese people's courage had created 'an atmosphere of self-satisfaction', while there were suggestions from a respected source within the Colonial Office that the history of the Second Great Siege should be re-written as,

> *...the Maltese have so exaggerated their own courage and endurance in this war, that there are only too many people itching to debunk them as soon as publishers are freed from the cloying hand of censorship.*

While Mussolini and Hitler had failed to subjugate the Maltese, Britain was quite happy to return things to the way they were before the bombs started falling, with Malta maintained as a colonial outpost from which the Royal Navy could police the Mediterranean. But, with Palestine about to explode and colonial influence in India waning, the Maltese weren't about to accept a return to what the British regarded as the status quo.

Elections were held in the summer of 1947 and the victorious Labour Party negotiated successfully with Whitehall for self-government. Maltese politics being what they are, however, a row soon broke out over funding to rebuild the island through the Marshall Aid programme, causing a rift between Party leader Dr Paul Boffa and his Minister of Works and Reconstruction Dom Mintoff. It eventually ended with Boffa leaving the Labour Party to form the Malta Workers Party and Mintoff succeeding him as General Secretary. But as far as the Royal Navy was concerned, it was still business as usual. Sailors still regarded Malta as one of their favourite drinking holes and Strait Street or Strada Stretta, known locally as' The Gut', regularly saw punch-ups among rival crews who had spent too long in the bars of Gzira and Valletta. 'The Gut' was also the capital city's red light district, though prostitution wasn't as prolific in Valletta as most sailors made out.

Dom Mintoff, meanwhile, was embarking on a political career that would see constant clashes with the British as well as his own people. Between 1950 and 1958, he fluctuated between being head of the

Shrapnel damage is still evident in Valletta's streets.

Legislative Assembly and leading the official opposition, heading talks in 1956 for integration of Malta into the British Parliament. But the move never materialised and by the end of the decade, relations between London and Valletta had broken down to such an extent that Mintoff resigned, swearing a pact of non-compliance, causing riots and a general strike that prompted the British to revoke the self-government treaty and place a Governor back in charge.

The 1960s saw Mintoff court further controversy, falling out with the Catholic Church who declared it a mortal sin to vote for the Labour Party. But the enigmatic social reformer survived the scandal and, after Malta was granted full independence in 1964, went on to oversee Malta become a republic in 1974 and the final British withdrawal in 1979.

Dom Mintoff, Malta's enigmatic social reformer.

Kalafrana, now under the auspices of the RAF, was the last British base to close on Malta and the island was free to court investment from world powers, which would have been frowned upon by the previous administration, China and Libya being two of the states that enjoyed a brief role as influential trading partners.

The emergence of the National Party in the 1980s saw Malta gradually move towards European integration, however, with the island state applying for full membership of the EU in 1990. In 1993, the Maltese themselves voted overwhelmingly to join the European Union and when then Prime Minister now President Eddie Fenech Adami signed the Accession Treaty in Athens in 2003, he officially made Malta trading partner and ally to several nations who, at one time or another, had tried to wipe his country off the map.

The journey will be complete when the Euro replaces the Maltese Lira on January 1st, 2008.

Chapter Twelve

Touring the Islands

TOURISM HAS BEEN THE PRINCIPAL INDUSTRY on Malta and Gozo since the 1960s, the islands' all-year temperate climate attracting visitors summer and winter. With EU funding, the island is even beginning to repair its notorious road network though potholes remain a hazard for anyone brave enough to hire a car, especially on the roads linking outlying villages. The best way to see Malta, however, remains the bus.

Though virtually all routes on Malta begin and terminate at Valletta, there is almost nowhere that can't be reached for a few cents on board one of the privately-owned vehicles which, contrary to popular belief, are now largely modern air-conditioned coaches that make travel a pleasant experience.

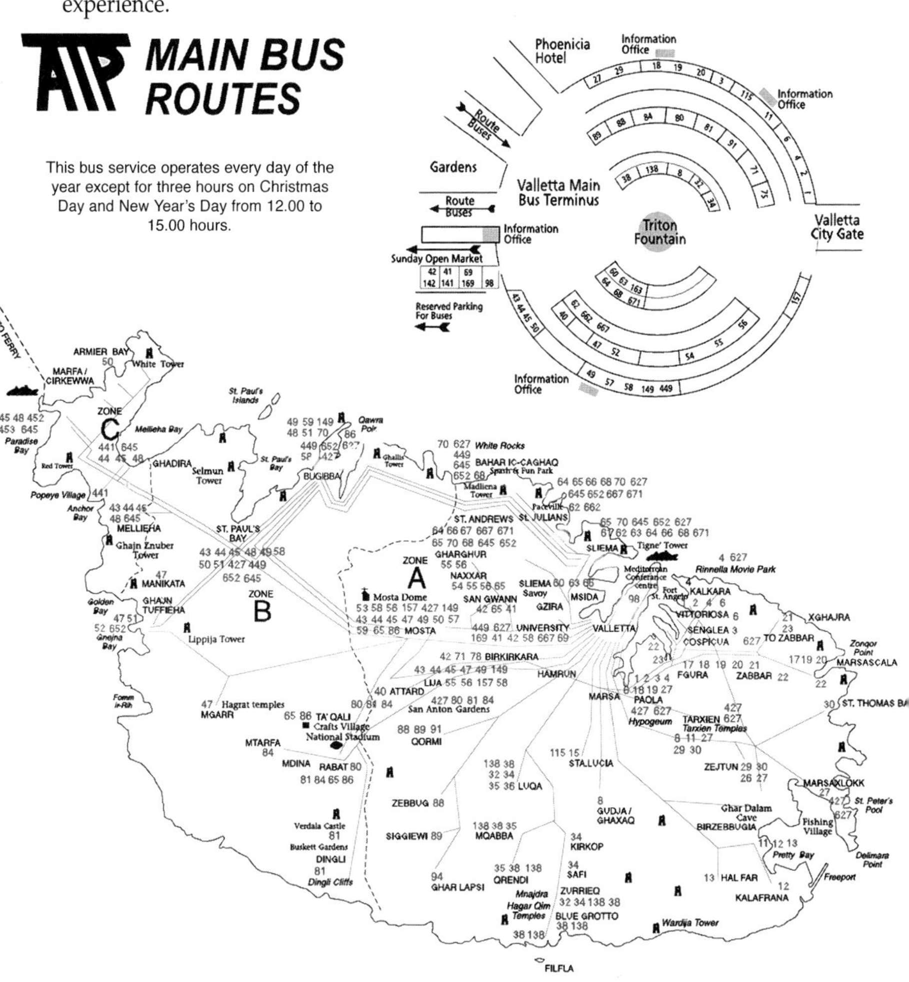

Getting to Malta has also never been easier, with many low-cost airlines operating frequent flights in summer from a variety of regional UK airports and major airlines, such as Air Malta and British Airways, running a scheduled service to Luqa at other times of the year. There's even a daily catamaran service from Sicily for non-fliers, while passenger and car ferries run regularly between Cirkewwa and Sliema to Mgarr on Gozo in all weathers.

Accommodation on the island varies from two to five-star, most of it based around St Julian's Bay, Bugibba and Sliema, though those preferring a more tranquil way of life may find resorts like Mellieha and Golden Bay more to their liking.

In recent years, Hollywood has also discovered that Malta has plenty to offer. Blockbusters including *Midnight Express*, *Gladiator*, *Troy*, *The Da Vinci Code* and *Alexander* have all used locations on the islands as well as utilising the state-of-the-art facilities of the Mediterranean Film Studios in Kalkara and history of course, both modern and ancient, is everywhere you look on Malta.

Lavish film sets on Malta.

VALLETTA, FLORIANA AND THE THREE CITIES

Begin with a harbour cruise

Valletta and the towns surrounding the dockyards bore the brunt of Axis aggression in WWII and, as such, this area probably has more to offer the visitor than other areas and the ideal way to start exploring Malta's capital is by boat.

The **Captain Morgan** and **Luzzu** harbour cruises set sail from **The Strand** in Sliema, immediately adjacent to the town's bus terminal. The cruises circle the former submarine base on Manoel Island and pass by some noteable landmarks including St Elmo's bridge, where the X Flotilla raid foundered and the docks where both the *Illustrious* and the *Ohio* were berthed. Guided tours of Grand Harbour and its environs are available throughout spring, summer and autumn.

Valletta

Entering the magnificent fortress city on the peninsula of Mount Sciberras on foot, most tours begin at the City Gate passing over the Great Ditch where the entrance corridors to a honeycomb of air raid shelters can still be seen. A walk down Republic Street passes by the bombed-out Opera House, St John's Co-Cathedral, Palace Square and the Grand Master's Palace, residence of former Governors and now home to the Maltese Parliament.

Houses and apartments on many streets leading off from Republic Street still carry evidence of shrapnel damage, but much of Valletta's waterfront is in the process of renovation, having been decimated during WWII, although several bombed-out buildings are still awaiting redevelopment behind the restaurants and shops of the new cruise terminal, alongside the Old Customs House.

Vittoriosa waterfront also suffered greatly during the Second World War but the Palace of the Prud'homme of the Arsenal survived the bombs, as did the ancient residence of the captain of the Galleys and the Caraffa Stores Building. However, war damage along here is still very much in evidence, especially close to the entrance to the new marina adjacent to the glamorous Casino di Venezia.

Fortifications

FORT ST ELMO **(Valletta V1 Map A)** guards the approaches to both Grand and Marsamxett Harbours and, once equipped with twin six pounder guns (the emplacements can still be seen), was the first target of the *Regia Aeronautica* in the Second World War. Continually strengthened since the Great Siege of 1565, nowadays it houses the National War Museum and is

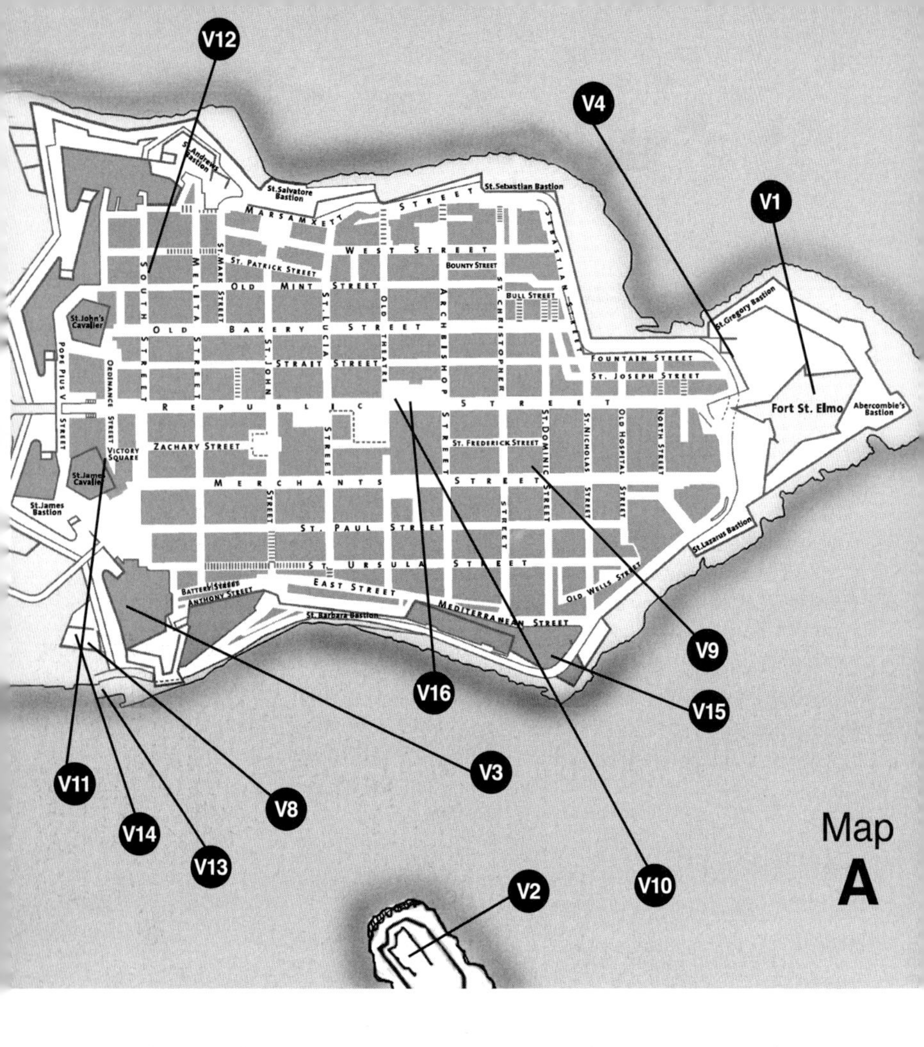

home to the Malta Police Academy. Historical re-enactments and military parades are also held throughout the year – see local advertisements for details.

FORT ST ANGELO **(Vittoriosa V2 Map A)** reputedly stands on the site of an ancient Roman settlement and was another prime target of the Italians and Germans during the Second World War. In 1912, the British Navy officially listed the fort as a ship (HMS *Egmont*) renaming it HMS St *Angelo* in 1933. St Anne's Chapel and the magisterial palace occupy the upper floors.

FORT RINELLA **(V3 Map B)** is a 19th century coastal battery built to house a massive 100-ton cannon. During the Second World War, it served as a lookout point for British forces and nowadays contains a museum focusing on life in a British garrison and containing military artefacts and ordnance.

Guides in historic costumes host tours of the battery every day except Sunday. **Bus nos. 1, 2, 4 & 6**

Contact: Fondazzjoni Wirt Artna
St Rocco Road
Kalkara CSP11
e-mail: info@wirtartna.org

FORT ST LUCIAN **(M1 Map C)**, built on the western shoreline of Marsaxlokk Bay, is a 17th century fortification that served as a munitions depot during the Second World War. Close to the gallant Breconshire's final resting place and overlooking the former flying-boat moorings at the now redeveloped Kalafrana, the fort is now home to the Malta Marine Research Centre. **Bus no. 27**

FORT CAMPBELL **(M2 Map C)** and the adjoining Sterling Barracks are one of Malta's best-kept secrets. Rare in that they were built specifically for use in WWII, barracks and gun emplacement sites remain largely intact, if a little overgrown, but some of the buildings are in a poor state of repair and

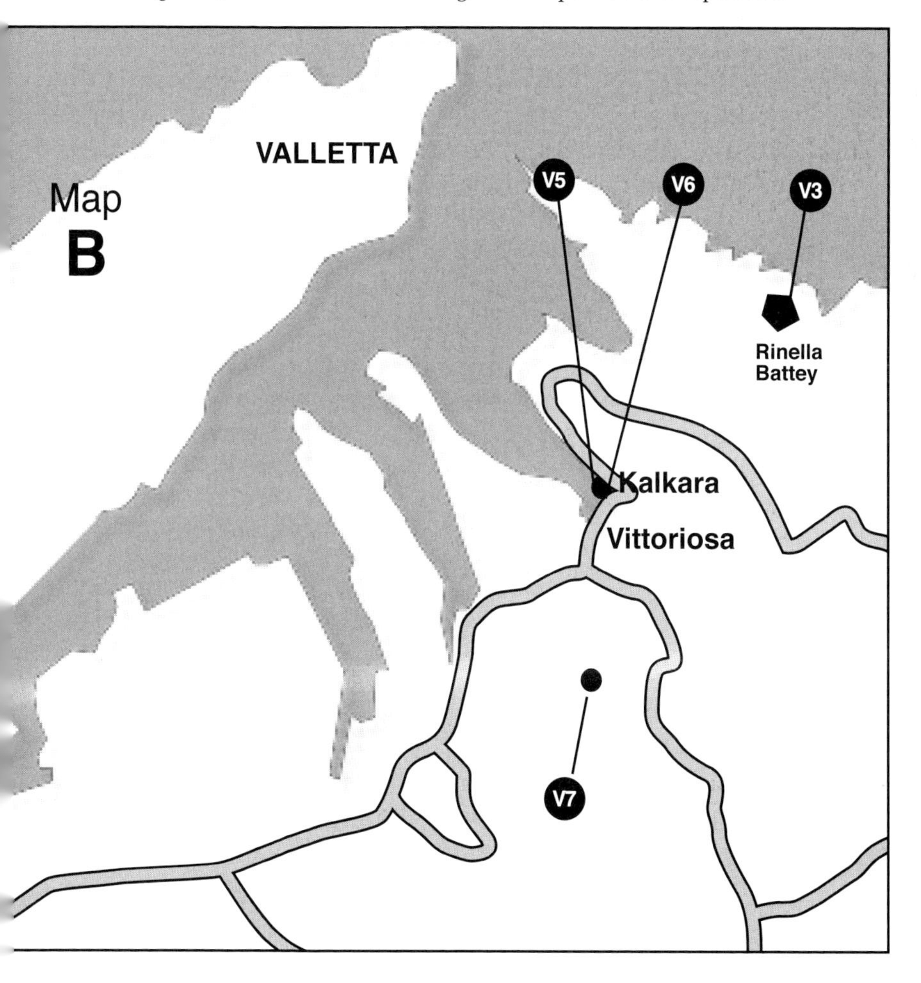

care is needed. Follow the signs for the Selmun Palace in Mellieha, the fort is approximately half-a-mile beyond the hotel overlooking St Paul's Island. **Bus no. 44**

Other sites worth a visit;

FORT ST LEONARDO, in Zabbar **(M4 Map C)**, features an 11-inch gun emplacement and buildings. **Bus no. 21**

DELLA GRAZIE BATTERY **(M3 Map C)**, currently undergoing renovation and development, stands on the shore to the east of Grand Harbour in the town of Xghajra. Access to the site, which features a sunken 10-inch gun emplacement, is across a causeway. **Bus no. 23**

MUSEUMS

LASCARIS WAR ROOMS **(V3 Map A)** in the Lascaris Bastions in Floriana was the centre of Mediterranean wartime intelligence gathering. Open to the public all year round and largely intact, displays depicting its wartime role are housed in its underground bunkers (see visitmalta.com for further details).

THE NATIONAL WAR MUSEUM in **Fort St Elmo (V4 Map A)** has an extensive collection of memorabilia, photos and documents from WWII including the remains of the Gloster Gladiator 'Faith', President Roosevelt's jeep 'Husky', an Italian X Flotilla E-boat, a Bofors anti-aircraft gun and Malta's famous George Cross. Open all year round.

Contact: National War Museum
Fort St Elmo
Valletta VLT 02
e-mail: info@heritagemalta.org

THE MALTA AT WAR MUSEUM in Vittoriosa **(V5 Map B)** includes a guided tour of a communal underground air raid shelter and the chance to view a film, commissioned to educate the British public, which includes actual footage of air raids and wartime life on Malta. A small bookshop is at the entrance and tours of Fort Rinella Battery can be included in the admission fee. Open all year except Bank Holidays. **Bus Nos. 1, 2 & 6**

Contact: The Malta At War Museum
Couvre Port Gate
Vittoriosa
e-mail: info@wirtartna.org

MALTA AVIATION MUSEUM **(M5 Map C)** is built on part of the site of the former RAF base at Ta'Qali. Exhibits include a MarkVI Spitfire, a Hurricane and a Fairey Swordfish as well as a collection of engines from WWII aircraft, uniforms and memorabilia. Restoration work on potential new exhibits is ongoing and can be viewed. Open daily except Bank Holidays. **Bus nos. 80, 81 & 84**

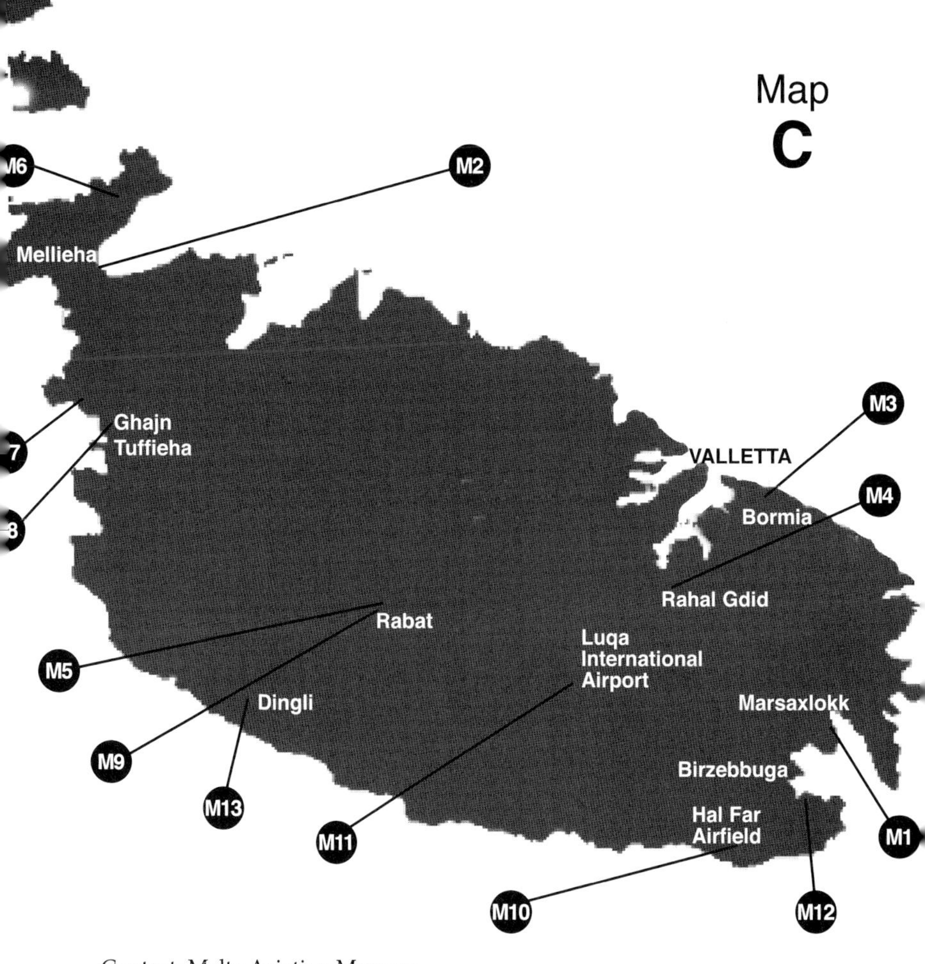

Contact: Malta Aviation Museum
Ta'Qali
RBT 13
e-mail: info@maltaaviationmuseum.com

MALTA MARITIME MUSEUM **(V6 Map B)** charts the islands' maritime history from ancient times to the modern day. Many of the displays in the main area focus on the influence of the Order of St John but a separate hall concentrates on Malta's role as a British naval base, with items and photos depicting military and civilian life. **Bus nos. 1, 2 & 6**

Contact: Malta Maritime Museum
Ex-Naval Bakery
Vittoriosa CSP 08
e-mail: info@heritagemalta.org

Other sites worth visiting:

NOTRE DAME GATE or Zabbar Gate **(V7 Map B)**, a five-storey gatehouse built into the Cottonera Lines in 1670 that guards Valletta from the south-east. It was strengthened in 1939 to act as an emergency bomb shelter. **Bus nos. 26 & 29**

The OLD SALUTING BATTERY **(V8 Map A)** can be found on the lower part of the St Peter And St Paul Bastion in Valletta. Used by the master timekeeper, the firing of a gun was used by ships and dockyard workers to mark the beginning and end of the working day. Now fully restored, volunteers, dressed in the uniform of the Royal Malta Artillery, take tours every morning.

Valletta's PALACE SQUARE **(V9 Map A)** is bordered by the GRAND MASTER'S PALACE, former residence of the British Governor. The opposite HOSTEL DE VERDELIN has a theatre showing archive film of the Second World War, while the walls in the square contain tablet quotations from King George VI and President Roosevelt.

THE OPERA HOUSE **(V16 Map A)** has been left partially standing as a monument to all the Maltese had to endure during the Second World War.

The AUBERGE DE PROVENCE **(V10 Map A)** on Republic Street housed the British Armed Forces Union Club until 1954 and the fully restored AUBERGE DE CASTILE **(V11 Map A)**, now the Prime Minister's Residence, was home to British Military HQ.

ADMIRALTY HOUSE **(V12 Map A)**, on South Street, was home to the British Naval Command until 1961.

OLD CUSTOMS HOUSE **(V13 Map A)**, opposite Dockyard Creek alongside Grand Harbour, is where the Italian Navy officially surrendered to Allied Forces in 1943.

UPPER BARRAKKA GARDENS **(V14 Map A)** in Valletta was the focal point for civilians gathering to greet the convoys. Offering the best view of Grand Harbour, the gardens overlooked one of the Royal Malta Artillery's key AA positions in the Second World War.

LOWER BARRAKKA GARDENS **(V15 Map A)** on the St Lazarus Curtain encompasses the Siege Bell and the Second World War Memorial as well as the monument commemorating the award of the George Cross.

CHURCH OF ST PUBLIUS **(V15 Map A)** in Floriana became an iconic image of wartime, refusing to close despite sustaining considerable damage.

ST AGATHA'S TOWER **(M6 Map C)**, also know as the Red Tower, can be viewed from the road linking Mellieha to Cirkewwa. Manned during both World Wars as a lookout post, the site is now a radar installation for the Maltese Armed Forces, so actual access in restricted. **Bus nos. 45, 452 & 453**

GOLDEN BAY **(M7 Map C)**, formerly Military Bay, was where Allied troops rehearsed for the Sicily landings and nearby GHAJN TUFFIEHA **(M8 Map C)** was a firing range for the British Army and Royal Marines.

The cliffs along this coast saw many commando exercises and a disused RM depot still stands on the site. **Bus nos. 47 & 52**

TA'QALI CRAFT VILLAGE **(M9 Map C)** still retains the identity of its former use as an airfield and many of the disused authentic buildings at the rear of the site have been largely left as they were when the RAF moved out. Concrete runways and taxiways, albeit shortened, are also still intact. **Bus nos. 80, 81 & 84**

HAL FAR **(M10 Map C)**, the former RAF airfield, is now a freight depot but administration building and former barracks remain in use at its entrance **(Bus no. 13)** with the site still adjoining the former RAF base-turned-international airport at LUQA **(M11 Map C). Bus no. 36**

KALAFRANA **(M12 Map C)** the site of the former seaplane base is now an expanding commercial port. **Bus no. 11**

DINGLI CLIFFS **(M13 Map C)** was the site of Malta's first radar. The Maltese Civil Aviation Authority have now moved in. **Bus no. 81**

Diving clubs, too, are now becoming popular on Malta and Gozo with the clear and normally calm waters of the Mediterranean offering perfect conditions to view the many wrecks that lie on the edge of the volcanic outcrop on which the islands sit. The remains of a crashed Bristol Blenheim and the hull of the HMS *Maori* which was sunk in Marsamxett Harbour in 1942, are just two examples of what is beneath the waves for the more

The remains of a crashed Bristol Blenheim beneath the Mediterranean. The clear waters make it ideal for divers to examine wartime wrecks.

adventurous to explore. Visit visitmalta.com for further details.

The Second World War has undoubtedly left a huge legacy on Malta and there are still reminders everywhere of what these islands went through. It's a sobering experience to visit the Military Cemeteries at Pembroke, Pieta, Mtarfa and Kalkara to understand the sacrifice the servicemen of the Commonwealth made in defence of the islands. There are also memorials to the fallen at Sliema, in Floriana and Ta'Qali as well as the symbolic Siege Bell overlooking Grand Harbour with its plaques of remembrance

The Capuchin Cemetery in Floriana and St Lawrence's Cemetery in Vittoriosa contain the graves of many of the civilians who lost their lives in the bombing – all are maintained to the highest standards and treated with the utmost respect.

But if you want to pay a lasting tribute to those who made the ultimate sacrifice, stand beneath the arches of the regenerated Upper Barrakka Gardens, look across Grand Harbour and try to imagine what the scene in front must have looked and sounded like under the bombs of the Regia Aeronautica and the Luftwaffe. Had the people of Malta and the airmen, soldiers and sailors of the island's garrison not stood up to be counted in those dark times – how different a world we would now be living in?

ACKNOWLEDGEMENTS

The Times Of Malta
The Imperial War Museum, London
Malta Aviation Museum
Royal Irish Rangers
www.navalhistory.com
www.visitmalta.com

Mobilisation In Action – Anthony Zarb-Dimech
Malta Convoys – David A. Thomas
The Air Battle For Malta – James Douglas-Hamilton
Raiders Passed – Charles B. Grech
The Siege Of Malta 1940-42 – David G. Williamson
Malta The Great Siege 1940-1943 – David Wragg
Hurricanes Over Malta – Brian Cull/Frederick Galea
When War Broke Out – Laurence Mizzi
Britain In The Mediterranean And The Defence Of Her Naval Stations – Quentin Hughes

Index